MTSS for Reading Improvement

A Leader's Tool Kit for Schoolwide Success

SARAH BROWN   STEPHANIE S

Solution Tree | Press

Copyright © 2025 by Solution Tree Press

Materials appearing here are copyrighted. With one exception, all rights are reserved. Readers may reproduce only those pages marked "Reproducible." Otherwise, no part of this book may be reproduced or transmitted in any form or by any means (electronic, photocopying, recording, or otherwise) without prior written permission of the publisher.

555 North Morton Street
Bloomington, IN 47404
800.733.6786 (toll free) / 812.336.7700
FAX: 812.336.7790

email: info@SolutionTree.com
SolutionTree.com

Visit **go.SolutionTree.com/literacy** to download the free reproducibles in this book.

Printed in the United States of America

Library of Congress Cataloging-in-Publication Data

Names: Brown, Sarah (Sarah Eleanor), author. | Stollar, Stephanie, author.
Title: MTSS for reading improvement : a leader's tool kit for schoolwide success / Sarah Brown, Stephanie Stollar.
Description: Bloomington, IN : Solution Tree Press, [2025] | Includes bibliographical references and index.
Identifiers: LCCN 2024050542 (print) | LCCN 2024050543 (ebook) | ISBN 9781962188814 (paperback) | ISBN 9781962188821 (ebook)
Subjects: LCSH: Multi-tiered systems of support (Education) | Developmental reading. | Educational leadership.
Classification: LCC LB1029.M85 B76 2025 (print) | LCC LB1029.M85 (ebook) | DDC 371.19/2--dc23/eng/20250213
LC record available at https://lccn.loc.gov/2024050542
LC ebook record available at https://lccn.loc.gov/2024050543

Solution Tree
Jeffrey C. Jones, CEO
Edmund M. Ackerman, President

Solution Tree Press
President and Publisher: Douglas M. Rife
Associate Publishers: Todd Brakke and Kendra Slayton
Editorial Director: Laurel Hecker
Art Director: Rian Anderson
Copy Chief: Jessi Finn
Senior Production Editor: Suzanne Kraszewski
Proofreader: Elijah Oates
Cover and Text Designer: Laura Cox
Acquisitions Editors: Carol Collins and Hilary Goff
Content Development Specialist: Amy Rubenstein
Associate Editors: Sarah Ludwig and Elijah Oates
Editorial Assistant: Madison Chartier

What Experts Are Saying About *MTSS for Reading Improvement*

"I highly recommend *MTSS for Reading Improvement*. As I read this book, I pictured MTSS team members taking critical action steps: carefully examining reading data for all students, determining gaps in schoolwide reading performance, analyzing current curriculum and instructional practices, and implementing a powerful Tier 1 schoolwide reading program while never departing from data-driven decision making. With this book as your guide, you will undoubtedly experience schoolwide reading success."

—Anita Archer, Author and Educational Consultant

"Built on the foundational belief that every student can learn given the right conditions, *MTSS for Reading Improvement* takes the layered nuances of building a robust, sustainable system of improvement at the district, school, and grade team levels and distills the complex work into attainable steps. Brown and Stollar provide clear, research-based guidance that is both practical and actionable. From the reflective questions that open each chapter to the real-world scenarios that allow the reader to envision application in their setting, every process is outlined and includes straightforward steps and considerations to complete the work efficiently. The appendices are full of concise, ready-to-use checklists, tools, data protocols, and agendas that support the work of every team, from grade level to district level. I recommend this book to support every stage of MTSS implementation, from beginning steps to fine-tuning a system already in place. This book should be required reading for anyone tasked with improving reading outcomes for all students. It is the immunization that prevents school systems from failing in their mission to support every student."

—Sharon R. Carter, Director of MTSS, Ceres Unified School District, California

"*MTSS for Reading Improvement* is a must-read for school, district, and state leaders who want to systematically improve reading outcomes for students. Brown and Stollar bridge the research on the science of reading and MTSS to draw a compelling picture of the path to continuous improvement. Moreover, their experiences working with leaders across the educational system are evident throughout the book. Any leader navigating the change required to improve reading outcomes within their MTSS will benefit from the practical strategies and tools the authors have refined in collaboration with real schools doing the work."

—Jose Castillo,
Professor of School Psychology and Codirector, Institute for School-Community Partnerships, Integrated Services, and Child Mental Health and Educational Policy, Department of Educational and Psychological Studies, University of South Florida

"In the rush to improve reading outcomes, schools often look for the perfect program, but even the best programs fail without an effective system behind them. Brown and Stollar bring MTSS to life through meeting templates, helpful charts, and real-world examples. Unsure if your school is over-testing? Their assessment audit will tell you. Struggling with unfocused team meetings? Their ready-to-use agendas keep discussions productive. Confused about what to do with all those data? Their simple protocols guide analysis and action. Leaders will find exactly what they need inside *MTSS for Reading Improvement*: practical tools that take the guesswork out of implementation. Every leader serious about improving reading outcomes needs this book."

—Anna Geiger, Author; Host, *Triple R Teaching*; Creator, the Measured Mom

"This book masterfully connects the framework of MTSS with the science of reading, providing a powerful tool kit for school leaders committed to enhancing student literacy; it is exactly what is needed right now in schools. By emphasizing the importance of data-driven decision making, continuous improvement, and tiered instruction, the authors highlight how MTSS can transform schools into environments where every educator and student thrives. The resource offers practical tools, including meeting protocols and reflection questions, to empower leaders to align instructional strategies with research and improve systems tailored to the needs of their staff, students, and communities. With a focus on real examples of effective implementation and decades of lessons learned, this book serves as an indispensable guide to navigating the complexities of educational systems and fostering a culture of collaboration and equity.

"What truly sets this book apart is its relentless pursuit of making reading improvement stick through actionable insights and a dedication to removing barriers that impede progress. Brown and Stollar have crafted a resource that celebrates the expertise of classroom teachers while empowering leaders to create the conditions necessary for effective reading instruction and intervention. Recognizing the need for context-specific implementation, the book bridges the gap between research and practice, offering a balanced approach to MTSS for reading improvement that fits the unique challenges of each school. This guide is an essential read for educators and leaders striving to advance literacy outcomes and transform the lives of their students through meaningful, systemwide improvement."

—Jennifer Glasheen,
State Director, North Dakota's Multi-Tier System of Supports (NDMTSS)
Director of Teaching, Learning, and Assessment, South East Education Cooperative (SEEC)

"This book is packed with accurate information explained clearly and paired with actionable steps. Busy school leaders will appreciate its efficiency. It gets straight to the point, providing the essential information and directives needed to lead your school in building a sustainable and effective system of reading support."

—Lindsay Kemeny, Teacher and Author

"There is no shortage of resources to help educators understand the science of reading and how it can be translated into instruction. This book takes it a step further, providing a much-needed road map for educators to make the science of reading a reality in their school by using an MTSS framework. The activities and agendas provided are fantastic and will serve as useful tools for teams of educators to reflect on their current systems and translate the book into meaningful action that benefits all students."

—Jon Potter, Senior Technical Assistance Consultant, American Institutes for Research

"This is perhaps the best-balanced resource available for implementing the science of reading within an MTSS framework. It answers most of the what and how questions, while offering just enough of the why to be both persuasive and actionable. The tone is approachable, and the structure mirrors effective instructional practice, with advance organizer questions, reflection prompts, and real-world application scenarios. It will be invaluable to leaders, schools, and districts looking to elevate their reading instruction.

"Nearly forty years ago, when we began shaping what is now known as MTSS, we understood the problems but lacked the tools to solve them. Brown and Stollar have spent decades helping to build and scale those tools. One of this book's great strengths is the wealth of implementation supports—developed, tested, and refined through real-world use. Whether you're just starting or well down the road, this work offers practical insight and ready-to-use protocols grounded in deep, lived experience. It speaks with a voice that invites, supports, and empowers.

"There's a refreshing clarity throughout. The content is rich but never overwhelming. The details are precise and purposeful. Each chapter begins with thoughtful, actionable questions and is filled with scenarios that make the work tangible. The message is consistent and compelling: prevention outperforms remediation, and precision—not complexity—is what moves systems forward."

—W. David Tilly, Retired Deputy Director, Iowa Department of Education

To all the dedicated teachers learning about evidence-based reading practices and working hard to improve reading outcomes for their students. And to the visionary leaders striving to make their work more effective and rewarding. Your commitment to excellence and unwavering support for our students' futures inspire us.

Acknowledgments

Our work would not be possible without the decades of learning and mentorship from the dedicated, generous colleagues with whom we have worked. We are profoundly grateful for the support and guidance of Randy Allison, Anita Archer, George Batsche, Kathy Bertsch, Doug Carnine, Mike Curtis, Judy Elliott, Kim Gibbons, Janet Graden, Jeff Grimes, Sharon Kurns, Margie McGlinchey, Dawn Miller, Louisa Moats, Brad Niebling, Madi Phillips, Rita Poth, Pam Radford, Alecia Rahn-Blakeslee, Dan Reschly, Ed Shapiro, Mark Shinn, and Dave Tilly. Your expertise and time have not only enriched our deep understanding of supporting reading change through an MTSS but have also reinforced our belief that by working together in a system, we can ensure that every child becomes a successful reader.

Solution Tree Press would like to thank the following reviewers:

John D. Ewald
Education Consultant
Frederick, Maryland

Janet Gilbert
Principal
Mountain Shadows Elementary School
Glendale, Arizona

Erin Kruckenberg
Fifth-Grade Teacher
Jefferson Elementary School
Harvard, Illinois

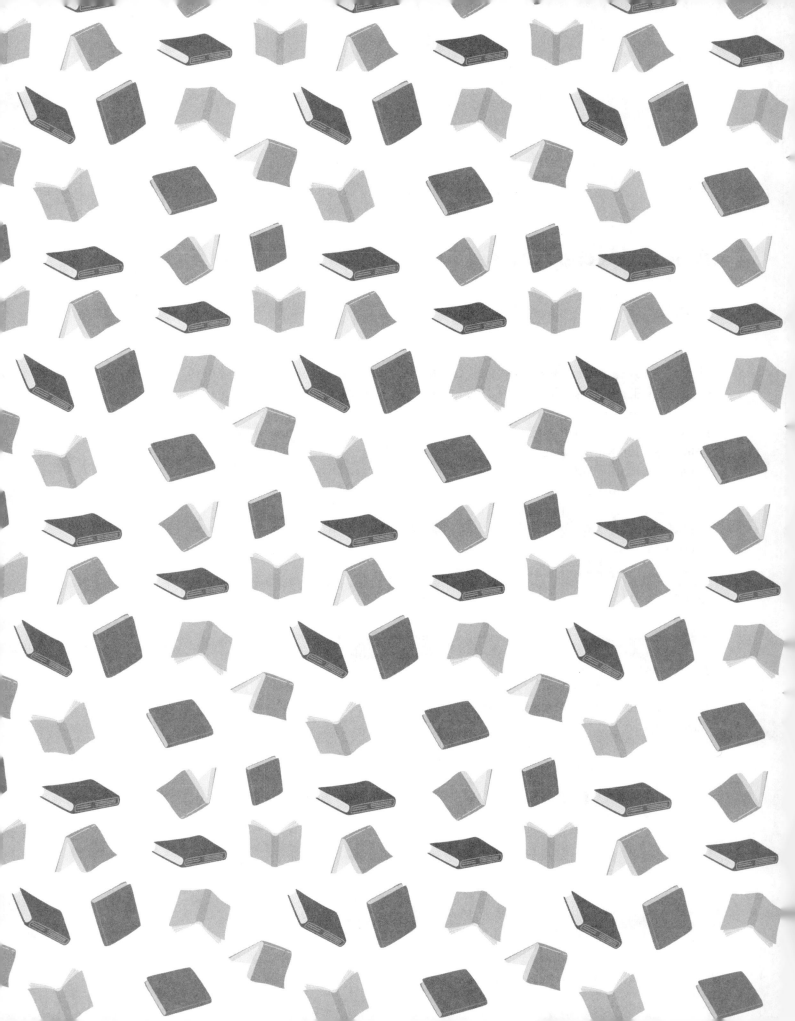

Table of Contents

Reproducibles are in italics.

About the Authors xiii

Introduction: Making Reading Improvement Stick 1
    A Multitiered System of Support (MTSS) and Reading Science: A Framework for Success . . 2
    Systems Matter: A System-Level and Student-Level Focus 4
    About This Book 5

Part I: Understanding Reading Science 9

1 Foundations of Learning to Read 11
    How Reading Research Informs What to Teach 11
    Applying Research in Practice 17
    Summary 17

2 Delivering Effective Reading Instruction 19
    What the Research Says About How To Teach Reading 19
    The Instructional Hierarchy 22
    Design and Delivery of Effective Fully Guided Reading Instruction 23
    The Leader's Role: Getting the Conditions Right 29
    Summary 30

3 Navigating Reading Assessment 33
    The Importance of Reading Assessment 33
    Assessment Purposes in MTSS 35
    Choosing Reading Tests 36
    Summary 43

Part II: Engineering a Robust System of Support 45

4 Foundations of MTSS 47
The Origins of MTSS 47
MTSS System Levers for Change 49
Use of Collaborative Improvement Cycle and the Connection to the Science of Reading . . 59
Summary 62

5 Teaming to Support Reading Improvement 65
The Importance of Teams in Enacting Reading Change 65
Teams and Their Functions 66
Collaborative Improvement Cycle to Support Teams 73
Common Teaming Challenges and Solutions 73
Summary 76

Part III: Enabling Educators to Improve Reading Outcomes 79

6 Using Data to Drive Tier 1 Reading Instruction for All Students 81
Grade-Level Team Conversations 81
Building Leadership Team Conversations 92
Summary 94

7 Using Data to Drive Tier 2 and Tier 3 Reading Instruction for Some Students 97
Reviewing Current Reading Outcomes: Gap Identification 97
Analyzing Gaps 99
Grouping 102
Action Planning 106
Gap Identification, Gap Analysis, and Action Planning in Building Leadership Teams . . . 106
Summary 107

8 Improving and Intensifying the Three-Tiered Model for Reading Results 109
Analyzing Results of Improvement Efforts 109
Using Both Student and Educator Data 110
Summarizing Outcomes of System-Level Reading Improvements 111
Intensifying System Supports 113
Identifying Lessons Learned in Intensification 115
Summary 117

Epilogue 119
Common Scenario 1 119
Common Scenario 2 120
A Final Activity 121
Summary 121

Appendices ... 123

Appendix A: Leader MTSS Tool Kit ... 125

A.1: Reading MTSS Reflection Guide ... 126
A.2: Elements of Explicit Instruction ... 131
A.3: Reading Tests Used ... 133
A.4: Building Reading Test Review ... 135
A.5: District Reading Test Plan ... 137
A.6: Reasons We Assess ... 139
A.7: Our Programs ... 140
A.8: Reading Instruction and Intervention Program Audit ... 142
A.9: Our Teams ... 143
A.10: Team Review ... 144
A.11: Team Communication Plan ... 147
A.12: Teams and the Collaborative Improvement Cycle ... 148
A.13: Tier 1 Discussion ... 149
A.14: Allocating Adult Resources ... 150
A.15: Intervention Selection Considerations ... 151
A.16: Intervention Scheduling ... 152
A.17: Comparing Intensity ... 153
A.18: MTSS World Café ... 154

Appendix B: MTSS Meeting Guide ... 155

B.1: Grade-Level Team Agenda Tier 1 ... 156
B.2: Grade-Level Team Protocol Tier 1 Gap Identification ... 158
B.3: Grade-Level Team Protocol Tier 1 Gap Analysis ... 160
B.4: Grade-Level Team Action Plan ... 162
B.5: Building Leadership Team Agenda ... 163
B.6: Building Leadership Team Protocol Gap Identification ... 165
B.7: Building Leadership Team Protocol Gap Analysis ... 167
B.8: Building Leadership Team Action Plan ... 168
B.9: Grade-Level Team Agenda Tiers 2 and 3 ... 169
B.10: Grade-Level Team Protocol Tiers 2 and 3 Gap Identification ... 171
B.11: Grade-Level Team Tier 2 and 3 Gap Analysis ... 173
B.12: Grade-Level Team Agenda Outcome Analysis ... 175
B.13: Building Leadership Team Agenda Outcome Analysis ... 177
B.14: Grade-Level Team Protocol Outcome Analysis ... 179
B.15: Building Leadership Team Protocol Outcome Analysis ... 181
B.16: Team Growth Reflection ... 182

References ... 183
Index ... 191

About the Authors

Sarah Brown, PhD, is President of System Impact Consulting. During her career, Sarah served in roles such as a professional learning leader in the ed tech assessment industry, bureau chief leading special education and MTSS implementation for the state of Iowa, district special education director, professional learning administrator, and school psychologist. Professionally, she's interested in the implementation of MTSS at multiple levels of the education system and improving systems to support high achievement for every student. She is coauthor of *Effective Universal Instruction: An Action-Oriented Approach to Improving Tier 1*. She earned her doctorate in school psychology from Northern Illinois University.

To learn more about Sarah Brown's work, visit systemimpcactconsulting.com.

Stephanie Stollar, PhD, is passionate about using MTSS as the framework for helping all students become skilled readers. She's an educational consultant and the founder of the Reading Science Academy, an online community where educators receive guidance to improve results in their schools. Stephanie supports states, nonprofits, and faculty to align the preparation of educators with the science of learning. She served as a vice president at Acadience Learning, provided training and consultation to hundreds of school districts, worked as an assistant professor of school psychology, and as a school psychologist. She earned her doctorate in school psychology from the University of Cincinnati. Stephanie believes that by supporting all educators, high achievement is possible for every student.

To learn more about Stephanie Stollar's work, visit www.readingscienceacademy.com.

To book Sarah Brown or Stephanie Stollar for professional development, contact pd@SolutionTree.com.

Ask Yourself...

- What are current reading priorities and initiatives in our district or school?

- Are there more students who need reading intervention than our system can effectively support?

- How are we providing ongoing support for reading improvement change efforts?

- How have we planned to use our MTSS to drive reading improvement?

INTRODUCTION
Making Reading Improvement Stick

If you've worked in a school, you know that they are incredibly complex organizations. Not only are the stakes high—We're preparing the next generation over here!—but there is too much to do, not enough time to do it, and barely enough people to keep it all going. We often spend so much time deciding what new things to implement that, by the time those conversations are finished, we have little energy left to devote to addressing how we'll establish and support the new practice over time. And, because schools are complex organizations (Kame'enui, Simmons, & Coyne, 2000), we often find that those new practices or tools fall to the wayside as plates fill up throughout the year (Lewis, 2015; McLaughlin, 1990). Despite knowing this, here we are, writing a book to support lasting reading improvement in schools because access to literacy is so important.

In our experience, sustaining change over time requires more than random acts of improvement. If your school is facing changes due to legislation promoting the science of reading or supporting students with dyslexia, we encourage you to carefully consider the context into which you are attempting to implement these new practices.

Maybe this sounds familiar to you: Your district spent time selecting a research-aligned reading program. Beyond the first few days of training and a follow-up meeting with the publisher, there was no plan in place to support the change. After all, you picked a good program. Teachers should be excited to run with it! However, in complex school contexts, there are a multitude of variables that can work against the effectiveness of that new program. Simply adopting an innovation such as a new reading program may not be successful if not supported by all aspects of the school system.

» Your universal screening tool may not provide information on how to match students to the new reading program.

» Teachers have been trained in balanced literacy approaches to reading instruction and do not have the background knowledge to effectively teach and differentiate using the new materials.

- » Teachers aren't sure which old practices to de-implement, and they attempt to add the new practices while also continuing to implement everything they were previously doing.
- » Parents are expecting the same old practices, such as sending home a spelling list or leveled reader, even though they aren't aligned to research.
- » District administrators believe adopting a new reading program is all that is required to implement the science of reading.

Improving reading outcomes by implementing the science of reading is not as simple as adopting a new program. If only it were so easy!

This book was born out of the recognition and respect for the unique and complex organization of schools and the knowledge that effective leadership impacts student outcomes (Carnine, 1999; Grissom, Egalite, & Lindsay, 2021; Kame'enui & Simmons, 1999; Murphy, 2004; Ringeisen, Henderson, & Hoagwood, 2003; Robinson, Lloyd, & Rowe, 2008). Our goal is to provide support to school leaders engaging in the important work of impacting reading outcomes in every classroom in a school. And while daunting, we assert that this is the right issue to tackle because every student is learning to read in the context of multiple overlapping systems. Each of those systems presents levers for change as well as potential barriers to success. Improvements in one part of the system will have intentional and unintentional impacts on other parts of the system (Curtis & Stollar, 2002). Our goal is to support school leaders to identify those variables and align all aspects of the system toward reading improvement.

A Multitiered System of Support (MTSS) and Reading Science: A Framework for Success

There's a field outside of education that studies why initiatives fail or succeed called *implementation science* (Fixsen, Blasé, & Van Dyke, 2019). Researchers in this field have determined that success requires evidence-based practice—like reading science—but that's not enough. Any new initiative must be contextualized so it fits with the unique needs and resources of the existing system. For example, the use of a comprehensive, cohesive, core reading program can improve reading outcomes. But which program is the best match to the needs of the students in your school, fits within your budget, works with your schedule, and will be implemented with fidelity by your educators? In addition, leaders must proactively support successful implementations for all educators within all classrooms. Having time and support for teachers to learn, not just when a program is first implemented but over time, is critical to experiencing consistent, systemwide implementation of new practices.

A multitiered system of supports (MTSS) offers a framework for implementing science-aligned reading instruction in a way that fits and even improves the system in which every student is learning to read. MTSS is a preventative framework in which schools use data to allocate resources to support all educators and students. It provides the vehicle to drive systemwide improved reading instruction that takes the science behind system change into account (Al Otaiba et al., 2011; Ervin et al., 2006; Harn, Chard, & Kame'enui, 2011; Vellutino, Scanlon, Zhang, & Schatschneider, 2008).

As schools identify a need to improve reading outcomes using research-aligned practices, a lot of attention is given to ensuring teachers understand this science and are using instructional routines that support learning to read and write. But new knowledge isn't enough. As school leaders work to plan for the implementation of these changes in classrooms, a framework for implementing and adjusting instruction is essential to success (Marzano, Waters, & McNulty, 2005). This allows for educators to have just-in-time resources to meet their needs.

We assert that the MTSS framework is the perfect choice for these efforts. In fact, The Reading League (2022) identifies *MTSS in the Science of Reading: Defining Guide* as the framework for implementing the reading research. MTSS is designed to flexibly meet the needs of local districts while ensuring critical educator and student needs are addressed. Through proactive strategies, regular data use, collaborative conversations, and responding to student needs through the flexible use of resources, the MTSS framework is the perfect companion to support schools working to improve reading outcomes.

When schools set priorities around reading improvement, looking to the research around teaching and learning related to reading is critical. This research, conducted consistently since the 1960s, informs how students best learn to read. When combined with the aligned context and implementation support that MTSS provides, implementation of the reading research has the potential to make lasting impact on local reading improvement efforts. Table I.1 contains definitions for both the science of reading and MTSS.

Table I.1: Defining the Science of Reading and MTSS

Term	Definition
The Science of Reading	"A vast, interdisciplinary body of scientifically-based research about reading and issues related to reading and writing. This research has been conducted over the last five decades across the world, and it is derived from thousands of studies conducted in multiple languages. The science of reading has culminated in a preponderance of evidence to inform how proficient reading and writing develop; why some have difficulty; and how we can most effectively assess and teach and, therefore, improve student outcomes through prevention of and intervention for reading difficulties." (The Reading League, 2022)
Multitiered System of Support (MTSS)	A multilevel prevention and intervention framework that uses data to support schools for resource allocation to address educator and student needs.

As a school change model, the MTSS framework can flex to meet many district priorities. For example, a school currently focused on improving reading practices and outcomes may receive information that the state department of education has a new requirement related to mathematics assessment. Because MTSS is an overall school improvement model, the framework can be used to support implementation of the new mathematics requirement, too. This flexibility allows leaders to spend less time creating new teams and planning supports and more time engaged in the critical work of implementing the change. In other words, MTSS is about building a more effective system.

Systems Matter: A System-Level and Student-Level Focus

Often, schools are tempted to approach MTSS in the way many approached response to intervention (RTI)—solely with the goal of identifying students who need additional support and creating interventions for those students. We suggest a different approach because, as we have seen in school after school in which we have worked, there are more students who need intervention than teachers and interventionists to support such a one-student-at-a-time approach.

Consider the second-grade team that meets to review their universal screening data and notices that 45 percent of students need intervention. They immediately know that there aren't enough intervention resources to support all these students and face tough decisions about which students will receive intervention. Do they limit who receives intervention? Do they provide interventions only to the readers who need the most help or to those who are closest to proficiency? None are a good (or right) choice. Then, once they decide who will receive intervention, they are faced with the inevitable awkward conversations with parents explaining why some students aren't receiving additional support. We don't want any school to have to engage in this frustrating process any longer.

Instead of focusing data use solely on individual student needs, we propose improving reading outcomes for all students through reviewing data for all students (aggregated data) to inform system-level decisions. When more than 20 percent of students perform below grade level, the intervention system is likely to be overwhelmed. Efforts to support individual students aren't very effective without systems in place for important functions such as knowing what students need to learn next (assessment systems), providing effective instruction (tiered instructional systems), scheduling and planning (teaming systems), and sustaining change over time (leadership systems). Throughout this book, we will provide tools for designing and implementing systems to deliver evidence-based reading instruction that gets results. The way forward is to focus on system-level implementation of the MTSS framework to drive reading improvement efforts.

System-level improvement is incredibly important for achieving better outcomes (Foster-Fishman, Nowell, & Yang, 2007). But when schools attempt to solve the reading crisis one student at a time their intervention system becomes diluted, and students with disabilities such as dyslexia can't get the intensive support to which they are entitled. We sometimes get so caught up in individual student needs that it can be challenging to find time to proactively plan for system support and address hurdles that arise to implementing the reading changes needed for improved student learning.

> MTSS is about building a more effective system.

In fact, system-level planning can dramatically improve learning trajectories for more students while better supporting educators along the way (Foster-Fishman et al., 2007). When schools use the Collaborative Improvement Cycle, which involves identifying, analyzing, and resolving barriers to reading success, they consider how to support groups of students and educators to meet their goals. Instead of reviewing individual student progress monitoring graphs, for instance, educators work in teams to review aggregate data on progress monitoring that provides information about how a group of students who received a similar instructional package (classroom reading instruction and reading intervention) are growing. This allows decision making at a group level and helps teams identify and plan to address system hurdles.

In a leadership in education podcast, Sharon Dunn, former principal at Loudon Elementary, discusses how she used MTSS to lead her school from roughly 30 percent of the students on track when they entered kindergarten to over 90 percent reading accurately at grade level at the end of sixth grade (Hamman, 2019). Similarly, in one school year, an instructional coach in Iowa implemented MTSS and Tier 1 intervention to grow from 29 percent of second graders meeting screening targets in the beginning of the year to 61 percent at the end of the year (Duncan & Brown, 2024).

We acknowledge that each grade level, and most classrooms, have individual students who need intensive, individualized programming; we do not intend to refute that. Yet it is impossible to provide effective intensive support to individual students when so many students are in need of reading support. We believe that the strongest impact on each and every student's reading skills is to have a school system that uses data regularly and collaborates to meet the needs of all students, including multilingual learners (MLLs), students with disabilities, and students who are high-achieving. The system that supports educators, in turn, supports students. That system has long taken a back seat to more urgent matters, and we're excited to shine a light on it and support leaders to focus on system improvement.

> System-level planning can dramatically improve learning trajectories for more students while better supporting educators along the way (Foster-Fishman et al., 2007).

About This Book

School leaders, including principals, assistant principals, school psychologists, instructional coaches, lead teachers, and interventionists who are in formal or informal positions of influence, will find the most benefit from this book. As we already mentioned, this book aligns with the research around lasting change in schools. It has three parts, each designed to address a critical component of system change. We believe that all three parts are essential to seeing lasting change within reading practices in a school, as informed by the science of implementation (Fixsen et al., 2019).

- » **Part I: Understanding Reading Science** focuses on the research related to the teaching and learning of reading and writing.
  - * Chapter 1 (page 11) provides critical background information about the science of reading.

- Chapter 2 (page 19) explores how instruction is critical to the success of reading improvement.
- Chapter 3 (page 33) introduces the types of assessment critical to using an MTSS to drive reading improvement.

» **Part II: Engineering a Robust System of Support** focuses on the local contexts that enable and support system change, including collaborative teaming and an overview of the MTSS framework.

- Chapter 4 (page 47) explores the MTSS and how a Collaborative Improvement Cycle drives MTSS implementation.
- Chapter 5 (page 65) describes the types of teams and collaboration that drive reading improvement and educator learning in schools.

» **Part III: Enabling Educators to Improve Reading Outcomes** focuses on the ongoing support through collaborative teaming that can occur through a school year to drive reading improvement with an MTSS.

- Chapter 6 (page 81) considers how to use reading data within an MTSS for all students within Tier 1 classroom reading instruction.
- Chapter 7 (page 97) implements data use within an MTSS for students accessing intervention supports in Tier 2 and 3.
- Chapter 8 (page 109) investigates the intensification of supports across all tiers when reading growth isn't sufficient.

We strongly believe that to make lasting reading improvement in schools, educators need ideas they can immediately implement, leaders need resources they can share and use right away, and teams need to be able to discuss important concepts deeply in a way that leads to action. Because of that belief, this book is organized to support leaders to take action. In each chapter we provide discussion on content, share anecdotes, and give actionable ideas. Additionally, each chapter has activities and tools that can be used in your building.

Activities for all educator meetings, grade-level teams, and building leadership teams also provide opportunities for further discussion and learning. These are provided in appendix A: Leader MTSS Toolkit (page 125). Resources like meeting agendas and data protocols guide the implementation of MTSS to support leaders to implement reading improvement systemwide. These are provided in appendix B: MTSS Meeting Guide (page 155). The appendix is separated into those two sections because we anticipate some teams may wish to print and share the entire MTSS Meeting Guide with their building leadership team while using specific activities and tools from the Leader MTSS Toolkit as priorities and needs arise.

To get started, we provide the "A.1: Reading MTSS Reflection Guide" that highlights key ideas for consideration (see appendix A, page 126). This guide is designed for teams to consider their current reading MTSS implementation and set priorities for using the

Continuous Improvement Cycle to support the work of district, school, grade-level, and student teams. In each row of the guide, you'll see corresponding chapters that are related to each item to drive teams toward additional resources that may help direct reading improvement efforts. Activities throughout the book provide instructions to use the appendix materials with teams. We encourage you to take full advantage of these resources and consider how they can support your team toward effective and efficient reading improvement. Start right now with the Building Leadership Team Activity in the feature box to the right.

We are eager to engage with you in thinking about how to effectively drive system improvement in reading for all students.

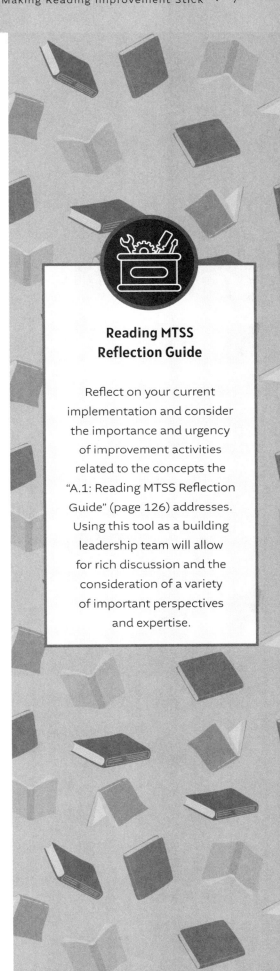

Reading MTSS Reflection Guide

Reflect on your current implementation and consider the importance and urgency of improvement activities related to the concepts the "A.1: Reading MTSS Reflection Guide" (page 126) addresses. Using this tool as a building leadership team will allow for rich discussion and the consideration of a variety of important perspectives and expertise.

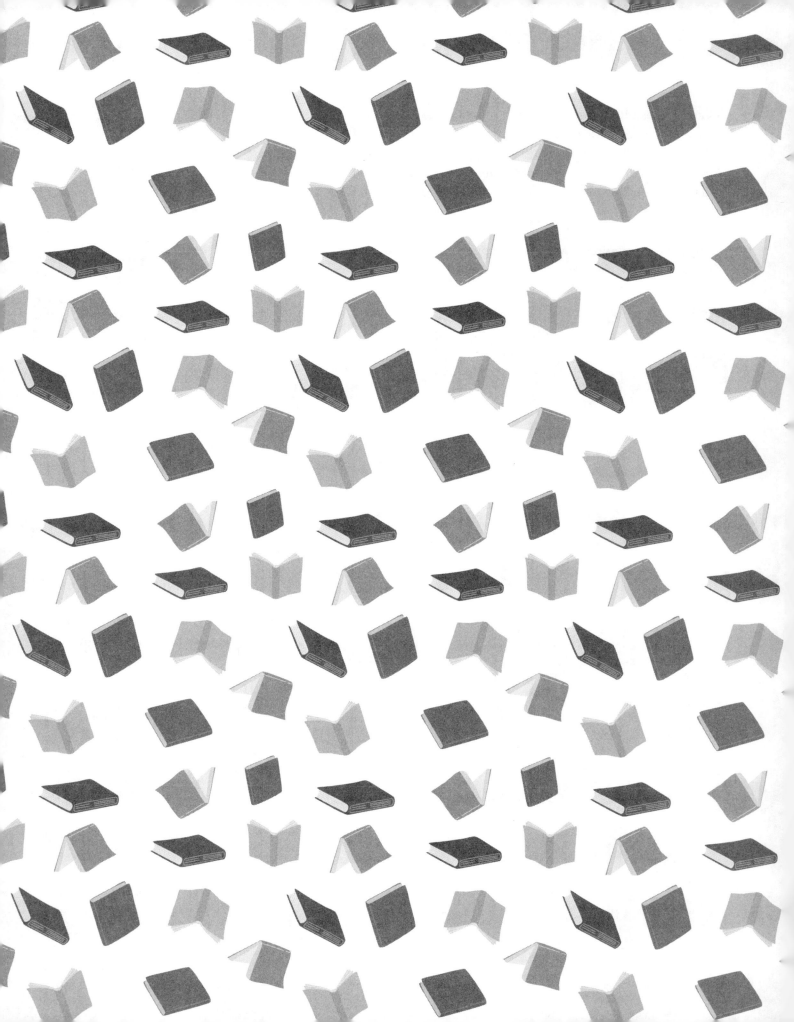

PART I

Understanding Reading Science

Ask Yourself...

- What are common knowledge and skills in our school around the science of reading?

- How well do all teachers in our school know the signs of reading difficulties?

- How do we make decisions about priorities for instruction?

- How are our reading instructional systems intentionally designed for prevention and early intervention?

CHAPTER 1
Foundations of Learning to Read

Now is a great time to improve reading outcomes. Never before has so much been known about how reading develops, what can go wrong during the process of learning to read, and how to organize schools to prevent reading difficulties and intervene if students struggle. None of this is easy, and research doesn't provide answers to all of our questions, but we have a solid research base that can inform our work (Castles, Rastle, & Nation, 2018).

Research involves asking questions and conducting experiments to reach conclusions. Basic research on reading by cognitive scientists, neurologists, psychologists, and others informs us about how the brain learns to read, how the brains of typical and struggling readers may differ, and how instruction changes the brain (Simos et al., 2005; Simos et al., 2007a; Simos et al., 2007b). Applied research done with students in real schools, under controlled conditions, using reliable and valid assessments of reading performance, and published in peer-reviewed journals offers guidance on what to teach and how to teach it (Castles et al., 2018; Foorman et al., 2016; National Reading Panel, 2000; Rose, 2006; Rowe, 2005; Vaughn et al., 2022; Wanzek et al., 2018).

How Reading Research Informs What to Teach

There are five foundational findings from the reading research that anchor this book. This chapter addresses the first three, and subsequent chapters address the final two.

1. Reading is not natural.
2. Prevention of reading difficulties is possible and more effective than intervention.
3. Reading comprehension is the product of word recognition and language comprehension.
4. Explicit instruction is more effective than implicit instruction. (See chapter 2, page 19.)
5. MTSS is the framework for implementing the science of reading. (See chapter 3, page 33.)

Reading Is Not Natural

No one is born with a reading brain. The connections necessary for reading are not present in our brains at birth; they must be built across time through experience and instruction (Dehaene, 2009). Unlike language, which is hard-wired into the human brain, reading is a newer human invention that has only been around for 1,500 or so years (Wolf & Stoodley, 2007). Babies learn to speak the language they hear around them without the need for direct instruction in how to talk. For many years, it was believed that reading worked in a similar way (Deheane, 2009; Seidenberg, 2017; Wolf & Stoodley, 2007). This led to a number of disastrous beliefs and classroom practices, several of which persist today, in spite of research to the contrary.

The faulty belief that reading will happen naturally when a child is developmentally ready has resulted in giving students "the gift of time" through counterproductive practices that include grade retention, waiting to start kindergarten, and taking a wait-and-see approach to early signs of difficulty. Over time, the number of students who need reading intervention increases, the caseloads of special educators become overloaded, and reading resources are stretched thin. In addition, there are long-term consequences for waiting to see if reading difficulties fix themselves. Research indicates that students who are old for their grade have a higher probability of negative outcomes such as school failure and dropout, drug use, teenage pregnancy, and involvement with the juvenile justice system (Goos, Pipa, & Peixoto, 2021; Jimerson, 2001; Rathmann, Loter, & Vockert, 2020; Van Canegem, Van Houtte, & Demanet, 2022).

The faulty belief that reading is a natural process also impacts our understanding of children who love to read. It is easy to observe that people who enjoy reading will choose to spend more time doing it. The co-occurrence of a love of reading and reading skill may have led to the faulty assumption that a love of reading is what produces skilled readers (van Bergen et al., 2022). It was long believed that the role of teachers in the primary grades was to get the conditions right for reading, surround children with books, model skilled reading, and vaguely foster this love of reading. In fact, some teacher training approaches argued against directly intervening by supporting students with reading difficulties because it would interfere with the natural course of development (National Association for the Education of Young Children, 2020).

Current research has gone beyond merely capturing the correlation between reading skill and enjoyment and now indicates that reading skill is what causes a love of reading, not the other way around (van Bergen et al., 2022). Students who leave first grade as struggling readers are very unlikely to catch up at a later point in time (Francis, Shaywitz, Stuebing, Shaywitz, & Fletcher, 1996; Juel, 1988; Torgesen & Burgess, 1998). Acting on this knowledge of the importance of prevention and early intervention is an essential component of MTSS. Given the evidence that reading is not a natural process, high-quality reading instruction becomes essential to preventing reading difficulties.

Prevention Is Possible and More Effective Than Intervention

One of the primary ways educational leaders can use the reading research to prevent reading difficulties is in guiding the selection of what to teach, when, and to whom. A vast body of evidence points to the need to select priority skills, sequence the skills in a general order, and then target instruction to meet students' needs within a tiered model of prevention and intervention (Castles et al., 2018). By using this information, schools can build a solid foundation of classroom reading instruction that meets the skill needs of emerging readers. For example, a teacher can teach digraphs explicitly and systematically (after prerequisite skills have been taught) during a scope and sequence, rather than teaching digraphs to all students and then providing intervention to those who didn't have the prerequisites to learn them.

Reading intervention is more expensive and less effective than prevention. For example, preventatively addressing a lack of phonemic awareness skills in kindergarten might take fifteen minutes each day across ten to twelve weeks, but intervening on phonemic awareness with a third-grade student might require hours of intensive instruction (Wanzek et al., 2018). Designing and delivering initial Tier 1 reading instruction in ways that align with the research on how students best learn to read has the ability to prevent the need to intervene with large numbers of students.

Reading Comprehension Is the Product of Word Recognition and Language Comprehension

Understanding what you read well enough to acquire knowledge through reading is the ultimate goal of reading instruction; however, to do so requires the use of several different skills. As professors Gough and Tunmer (1986) explain in their "Simple View of Reading," reading comprehension depends on two broad capacities: word recognition and language comprehension (Gough & Tunmer, 1986; Hoover & Gough, 1990; Hoover & Tunmer, 2018; Hoover & Tunmer, 2022). *Word recognition* means accurately and automatically recognizing words. *Reading comprehension* and *language comprehension* are the same in that they both involve gaining and making meaning, yet they are different in that one involves gaining meaning from speech (language comprehension) and the other from print (reading comprehension). Word recognition and language comprehension are separate capacities, and both are required for reading comprehension. In fact, Gough and Tunmer's (1986) simple view of reading is depicted in multiplication form because no amount of one capacity can compensate for diminished skills in the other.

Word Recognition (WR) × Language Comprehension (LC) = Reading Comprehension (RC)

The simple view of reading offers a useful schema for guiding what to teach and how to teach reading. Key ideas include the following.

> » All students can receive explicit and systematic instruction in word recognition and language comprehension from the first day of kindergarten.

» Before students have mastered word recognition skills, their language comprehension instruction occurs primarily through the teacher reading aloud from complex texts and facilitating discussion.

» Once students can read grade-level text accurately and fluently, the focus of instruction shifts to reading comprehension.

» When older students have difficulty understanding grade-level text, it is because they lack word recognition, language comprehension, or both.

Within the word recognition and language comprehension domains are subskills that serve as priorities for reading instruction, assessment, and intervention. The report by the National Reading Panel (2000) summarizes the research on the essential skills required for skilled reading. Since the report was released, research confirms the essential nature of the five skills—(1) phonemic awareness, (2) phonics, (3) vocabulary, (4) text reading fluency, and (5) reading comprehension (Castles et al., 2018; Foorman et al., 2016; National Reading Panel, 2000). In addition, there is recognition of the importance of writing, which some educators think of as a sixth essential literacy skill. Table 1.1 defines each of the five skills.

Table 1.1: Five Essential Reading Skills

Essential Literacy Skills	Definition
Vocabulary	Understanding the meaning of words we speak, hear, read, and write
Phonemic Awareness	Noticing, thinking about, and working with the smallest units of spoken language, which are called *phonemes*
Phonics	Knowing relationships between sounds (phonemes) and letters (graphemes) for reading and spelling
Reading Fluency	Reading connected text accurately, fluently, and for meaning
Reading Comprehension	Gaining meaning from text

Source: National Reading Panel (2000)

Reciprocity Among the Essential Skills

Although the essential skills are often depicted in a list, recognizing the reciprocal nature of the skills has great value. For example, some amount of phonemic awareness is needed for phonics, but once students learn to read and spell, they are able to do more advanced phonemic awareness skills such as adding, deleting, and substituting phonemes (Ehri, 2020). The same is true for the relationship between fluency and comprehension. A base level of text-reading fluency is required for reading comprehension, and understanding what is read increases fluency (Klauda & Guthrie, 2008). The best reading programs capitalize on this reciprocity by integrating across the essential literacy skill areas. For example, exemplary programs integrate the teaching of phonemic awareness and phonics, phonics and spelling, and writing and reading comprehension within their lessons.

Essential Skills Sequence

Essential literacy skills should be taught in an integrated fashion with an emphasis on a general progression from phonemic awareness and phonics, to reading fluency, to reading comprehension, with instruction in vocabulary and oral language throughout. See figure 1.1.

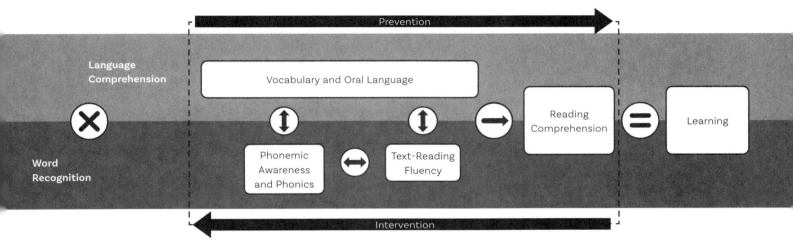

Figure 1.1: Reading skill progression.

Although the skills are reciprocal, there will be a shift across primary grades in the skills that teachers emphasize as the priority for mastery. For example, kindergarten students aren't expected to read for meaning, and instruction in phonemic awareness isn't typically needed for all students after first grade. In kindergarten, the curriculum focuses a larger proportion of time on phonemic awareness and alphabet knowledge because those skills are essential during early reading development. However, after first grade, a shorter percentage of reading time is allocated to those skills because most students have mastered them. The curricula in third grade and above tend to focus on reading comprehension because students are expected to have acquired the word recognition and text reading fluency skills that make reading comprehension possible. And, in all grade levels, focus on oral language, vocabulary, and knowledge building are always a priority.

What about grade-level standards? Literacy standards articulate the instructional outcomes that students should achieve by the end of each grade. Before designing instruction or assessment based on state standards, educators might ask themselves the following questions.

» To what extent do the standards align with research about what to teach?

» Are there some standards that research suggests are more important than others?

» Are the standards sequenced in order (simple to complex, prerequisites clearly noted) across the school year?

Standards tell us what learning teachers are trying to help students achieve, and curricula helps them get there. Standards aren't usually specific enough to build a scope and sequence from, so school and district leaders need to use research to define the scope and sequence. Then, grade-level teams use knowledge of research to decide *how* to approach state-required standards (such as read alouds versus student reading, and so on).

The following Lead to Succeed example shows how a grade-level team may consider the alignment and sequencing of skill instruction.

LEAD TO SUCCEED
Continuous Improvement

Your first-grade building leadership team reviewed data after the beginning-of-year screening and noticed that, after an initial improvement two years ago, the percentage of students on track with phonemic awareness was not continuing to grow. You decide to dig in more deeply, and through reading a research article and consulting with your speech-language pathologist, you realize that the phonemic awareness program you purchased two years ago may not be entirely aligned with research. Based on this information, your team decides to use the program flexibly and link phonemic awareness to the phonics and spelling lessons.

—

Given this rather large change, there are several things the building leadership team can do in this scenario to help build consensus for continuing to improve reading instruction.

- Share the research article with all staff and hold an optional after-school session to discuss what they learned and why the decision was made.

- Write a special newsletter to teachers explaining the decision, why the team made it, and emphasizing the goal of prioritizing improving reading outcomes over rigid adherence to board-adopted materials.

- Use the same content and materials in grade-level team meetings to discuss the decisions. The principal and speech-language pathologist join each of those grade-level meetings to reinforce support for the decision and to tackle any uncomfortable conversations that arise.

- Have an instructional coach or other educator model integration of the phonemic awareness routines with the phonics and spelling program and offer to observe and support implementation by classroom teachers.

Effective teams don't need to do all of these things, but supporting two-way conversations when significant change is implemented can help build consensus, and thus, systemic implementation of new practices.

Reflect and Connect

1. What opportunities exist for reflecting on the effectiveness of current programs and materials?

2. Which staff members have deep knowledge of reading research and can access journal articles to stay aware of new research?

3. How are decisions made about purchasing new instructional materials?

4. What are you doing to prioritize a focus on student outcomes rather than rigid adherence to programs with fidelity?

Applying Research in Practice

There are several ways school leaders can foster the application of research to practice.

- » **Intervene early:** Act at the earliest sign of student difficulty. Don't delay intervention. Screen students and then act at the beginning of kindergarten and as soon as possible in every grade. Advocate for providing or expanding programming for preschoolers in your district and community.

- » **Prioritize oral language:** Recognize oral language as the foundation of reading. Promote language comprehension urgently, explicitly, and simultaneously with word recognition. Honor and build on the spoken language of multilingual English learners and speakers of English variations when teaching reading.

- » **Focus on the essential skills:** Prioritize the essential literacy skills as nonnegotiable learning targets for all students. Teach in a general progression from easier to harder while also acknowledging the reciprocal nature of the skill areas. Reconcile and integrate the essential skills with grade-level standards.

- » **Integrate across essential skills**: Take advantage of the reciprocal nature of the five essential skills by integrating instruction across components (for example, teaching the meaning of words the students are segmenting, writing new vocabulary words, and asking a simple question after reading decodable text). Avoid rigidly breaking up the literacy block into separate skill units.

Summary

The vast body of knowledge referred to as the science of reading provides educators with actionable information about the essential skills that should form the basis of reading instruction in elementary grades. When teachers are aware of the importance of these skills and how they work together to result in students' reading comprehension skills, they can make better choices about how to spend precious time in the classroom. Also, educators with deep knowledge of reading science may be more likely to recognize reading difficulties in students early enough to change futures, approach reading intervention with a sense of urgency, and design instructional systems that meet the needs of all students. Use the "A.1: Reading MTSS Reflection Guide" (page 126) to identify the training and coaching on reading research that your team needs.

Ask Yourself...

- What do we know about the research on how to teach beginning and struggling readers?

- In our school, how do educators decide the instructional strategies that will best meet students' learning needs?

- How are the essential elements of explicit instruction used consistently throughout our school?

- How does our district make decisions about instructional materials and routines?

CHAPTER 2
Delivering Effective Reading Instruction

Of all the many factors that influence reading outcomes, how reading is taught may be the one factor that is most within the control of teachers and school leaders. Teachers are faced with thousands of instructional decisions every day. In our experience, when school leaders create an instructional system focused on the principles of effective instructional design and delivery, teachers are more likely to use teaching that is aligned to the research and gets results.

In the previous chapter, we explored what the research indicates about effective instructional design, including decisions about which skills to teach, the order in which to teach the skills, and how to identify the right skill to teach each student at any point in time. This chapter explores aspects of effective instructional delivery, including selecting the right approach to teaching given what is most likely to work for all students and then customizing for each student based on their needs.

This chapter supports school leaders with background knowledge and action steps for improving the quality of reading instruction in their MTSS.

What the Research Says About How To Teach Reading

The debate about how to teach reading has been so long-standing and fierce that it has been referred to as a war (Castle, Rastles, & Nation, 2018). At the heart of the "reading wars" is the tension between those who believe everyone learns best when they discover or construct some or all of their own knowledge (constructivist learning) and those who believe learners with different levels of knowledge need specific guidance and support. In constructivist approaches to reading instruction, teachers provide minimal guidance. Their role is to facilitate the emergence of what are thought to be natural reading skills. One potential explanation for why this debate persists, well past the accumulation of scientific evidence to settle it, is that educators have confused the constructivist theory of learning with how reading should be taught (Kirschner, Sweller, & Clark, 2006).

> Of all the many factors that influence reading outcomes, how reading is taught may be the one factor that is most within the control of teachers and school leaders

In constructivist approaches, sometimes referred to as "student centered" approaches, large portions of reading instruction involve students doing self-guided activities at centers and being exposed to large numbers of books. Explicit instruction of word recognition skills is not prioritized—it is believed that most students will learn to read well without that explicit instruction and that such instruction may, in fact, hinder learning and a future love of reading.

By contrast, in a teacher-directed or behaviorist approach to reading instruction, educators focus a significant portion of each reading lesson on explicitly teaching word recognition skills in a structured manner. It is believed that joy for reading develops when students are proficient readers. In general, we enjoy things we are confident at doing.

Minimally Guided Approaches

Some educators argue that minimally guided instruction (called *problem-based learning, discovery learning, inquiry learning,* and *student-directed instruction*) is best in all subjects at all times (Steffe & Gale, 1995). They believe the teacher's role is to be a guide who gets the conditions right for learning but shouldn't directly intervene in what is thought to be natural development. They believe minimal guidance is superior or somehow more advanced because it allows students to create, construct, and direct their own learning. In reading, teachers who believe in minimally-guided approaches focus on creating environments that support reading (Australian Children's Education and Care Quality Authority [ACECQA], n.d.; Strong-Wilson & Ellis, 2007), like establishing a print-rich environment, having comfortable spaces to read around the room, and providing lots of books for students to choose from during reading lessons.

Fully Guided Approaches

Fully guided approaches involve directly and explicitly teaching reading and writing so learning is not left to chance. Explicit instruction involves fully guiding the learning through teacher actions such as breaking complex tasks into smaller units, sequencing new concepts and skills from easier to harder, directly stating or modeling what students should learn, providing immediate corrective feedback, cumulatively reviewing over time, and teaching to mastery.

Proponents of explicit instruction argue that direct, fully guided instruction is best when students are learning new skills or have a history of difficulty with the subject area, and when not learning the skills would have catastrophic consequences, such as when learning to read (Mayer, 2004; Sweller, 2003). They favor instruction that starts as direct and highly supportive and becomes less so as students acquire the new skills. The teacher's role is to carefully control the learning environment, preventing errors or responding to them with immediate correction. Prevention and early intervention are prioritized. When teaching reading, teacher-directed approaches would focus on the teacher addressing a specific scope and sequence of reading skills, with those lessons involving teacher-directed instruction, frequent student responses, and teachers correcting student errors immediately.

Research on Minimally Guided and Fully Guided Approaches

While both approaches seem like they may be valid ways of teaching reading on the surface, controlled experiments conducted with a variety of students in a variety of subject areas across decades confirm that direct, explicit instruction, with the opportunity to practice to mastery, is more efficient and effective when teaching new information to novices than minimally or partially guided instruction (Mayer, 2004). Two areas of research can guide school leaders to adopt, support, and sustain instructional approaches that have a greater likelihood of getting all students to be readers: (1) research on human learning and (2) research that compares the two approaches (Clark, Kirschner, & Sweller, 2012).

Research on Human Learning

Research in cognitive science reveals the functions of working memory and long-term memory and the ways they interact. The goal of all reading instruction is to cement new information to long-term memory, where there is unlimited storage capacity, making information available for instant and effortless retrieval in the future. Information is stored in long-term memory only after it is processed in working memory, which has very limited capacity (Sweller, 2016).

When novices receive a problem to solve, and they don't have background information to draw on, all they can use is their limited working memory. When there are no relevant concepts or procedures in long-term memory to draw on, working memory becomes burdened, and storage in long-term memory is unlikely (Chen, Castro-Alonso, Paas, & Sweller, 2018). For example, when first-grade students are asked to discuss, conference with a teacher about, or write about what they read, they may remember very little of the content if they had to struggle to sound out every word of the text.

Novices can spend a great deal of time engaged in problem solving, group projects, or discovery and not commit any new information to long-term memory (Clark et al., 2012; Sweller, Mawer, & Howe, 1982). Therefore, careful consideration should be given to when it is appropriate to ask students to work independently to apply, transfer, and generalize knowledge to novel, challenging, or ambiguous tasks.

Beginning readers are novices whose learning can be efficiently supported by teachers who carefully present new information, connect it to what is already known, and work with students to practice new skills to a level of mastery that facilitates application, transfer, and generalization. Once students have acquired expertise in reading—they can read text accurately and fluently—we can expect them to engage in minimally guided reading activities such as reading text independently and applying their reading skills to tasks such as discussion and writing.

Research Comparing the Approaches

Research studies that compare minimally guided and fully guided approaches to reading instruction consistently confirm the superiority of teacher-directed instruction for beginning and struggling readers (Mayer, 2004; Moreno, 2004). A variety of problems, as detailed here, consistently occur when minimally guided instruction is used with novices (Moreno, 2004).

- » Students who have a lot of background information and skills are the only ones who learn with minimal guidance.
- » Students without the background information become frustrated, copy from their peers, check out during instruction, make mistakes, and acquire misunderstandings, which they must later unlearn.
- » Students working in groups take longer to acquire the new knowledge and skills.

Although there is no research that finds that minimally guided approaches to teaching reading are more effective for teaching beginning and struggling readers, estimates of the use of these approaches indicate they are used frequently in the form of programs such as Guided Reading and Reading and Writing Workshop (California Reading Coalition, n.d.; Martin & McLarren, 2023; Ohio Department of Education & Workforce, 2024). Savvy school leaders can navigate the tension between minimally guided and fully guided reading instruction by understanding when to use each approach.

Beginning and struggling readers clearly benefit from fully guided instruction, while expert readers can benefit from less guided instruction; therefore, minimally guided instruction has its place in reading instruction. What is important is the match between students and instruction. Learning will be limited if students are expected to act like reading experts too soon. On the other hand, learning can be accelerated by carefully matching the instructional approach to students' proficiency in the essential literacy skills.

The Instructional Hierarchy

The *instructional hierarchy* (Haring & Eaton, 1978; VanDerHeyden & Burns, 2023) is a helpful framework for determining the right time for students to engage in student-directed learning (table 2.1). When people learn new information, they initially perform new tasks slowly and make many mistakes. Students who are learning new information need direct and supportive instruction that promotes correct responding. This is called the *accuracy phase*.

With sufficient practice and repetition, students move into the fluency phase, where the new skill moves from something that is done accurately to something that is done effortlessly and fluently. At that point, performing the skill or accessing the information has become unconscious and available for effortless retrieval to apply to the kinds of novel and complex problems, situations, and tasks expected in minimally guided learning during the generalization and transfer phase.

Let's take an example of how the instructional hierarchy applies to learning word recognition skills. First, students must acquire and accurately perform new skills such as segmenting phonemes, matching phonemes to graphemes, reading and spelling words, and accurately reading text. Next, students must over-learn those new skills so they are

Table 2.1: The Instructional Hierarchy

Phase of Learning	How Student Responses Look	Goal of Instruction	Ideal Instructional Approach
Accuracy	Slow and incorrect	Correct responses	Fully guided
Fluency	Slow and correct	Correct, automatic, and fluent responses	Fully guided
Generalization and transfer	Fluent = correct and automatic	Application of skill and knowledge to problem solving in a wide range of settings and materials	Fully guided Minimally guided

stored in long-term memory for fluent and effortless spelling and text reading. Finally, students can use their fluent text reading as the basis for group discussions, writing across sources, and solving novel problems.

Fully guided approaches work best when students are in the acquisition and fluency phases. Minimally guided approaches are appropriate when students are in the generalization and transfer phase. Reading instruction can be more effective and efficient when it aligns with where each student is on the instructional hierarchy. Learning will be limited when students are asked to apply skills and knowledge with which they are not yet fluent, or when they are asked to perform skills quickly that they aren't yet performing correctly.

School leaders, teachers, and other educators can deliver effective reading instruction when they know the differences between minimally guided and fully guided approaches to reading instruction, are aware of the phases of the instructional hierarchy, can identify the phase each student is in, and match the phase to the appropriate approach.

Design and Delivery of Effective Fully Guided Reading Instruction

Just because the teacher is guiding the instruction doesn't mean it will necessarily be effective. The following elements of effective instruction, compiled from various sources (Archer & Hughes, 2011; Luccariello et al., 2015; Paschler et al., 2007; Rosenshine, 2012; Willingham, 2009), provide criteria on which to base the selection and enhancement of instructional programs and approaches and the background knowledge necessary to observe and offer feedback on the delivery of reading instruction.

Although the following elements of effective instruction are not specific to reading, it is essential that reading instruction is carefully designed and delivered in the accuracy and fluency-building phases, especially for students who are just learning to read and for older struggling readers. Following are the characteristics of reading instruction that school leaders should look for when selecting materials for classroom and intervention instruction, approving professional development, working in teams to design and evaluate instruction and intervention, and observing in classrooms.

> Just because the teacher is guiding the instruction doesn't mean it will necessarily be effective.

> Although the following elements of effective instruction are not specific to reading, it is essential that reading instruction is carefully designed and delivered in the accuracy and fluency-building phases, especially for students who are just learning to read and for older struggling readers.

- » Organize the instructional environment
- » Present very little new information
- » Open lessons clearly
- » Break down complex information
- » Sequence content purposefully
- » Promote active engagement
- » Require frequent responses
- » Practice to mastery

Organize the Instructional Environment

Students learn best in classrooms that are consistent and when teachers demonstrate clear, high expectations, establish trust, and command and demonstrate respect (Cheryan, Ziegler, Plaut, & Meltzoff, 2014).

Teachers set the stage for learning by arranging the physical environment and using consistent routines. When students of all ages are learning new and important skills directly from the teacher, such as during reading instruction, the room should be arranged with desks in rows facing the teacher. The separation of desks minimizes distraction and increases time on task (Wannarka & Ruhl, 2008). With everyone facing the teacher, the teacher can easily scan the room to observe student responses and circulate to provide individual feedback. Figure 2.1 shares a depiction of this layout.

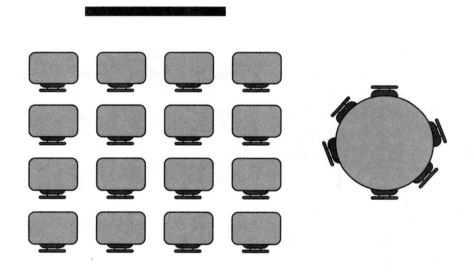

Figure 2.1: Optimal classroom organization for reading instruction.

Present Very Little New Information

Each lesson should primarily review previously learned content, with only about 10–20 percent new information. Remember that new information is learned in the context of what is already known (Carnine, Silbert, Kame'enui, Tarver, & Jungjuhann, 2006).

Most lessons begin with review and practice of previously taught material. As illustrated in table 2.2, in each lesson, a small amount of new information is presented in a way that connects it to what is already known, thus minimizing the demands on working memory and allowing time for enough practice to overlearn the new information and cement it in long-term memory.

Table 2.2: Sample Word Recognition Lesson Framework

	Component	Purpose	What It Looks or Sounds Like
1.	Opening of the lesson	Gain attention Clearly set the purpose	"Today, we will practice sound spellings that we've already learned and learn a new one."
2.	Review of previously taught material	Actively engage students in demonstrating what they do and do not remember from previous lessons	The teacher writes previously learned letters on the board and says, "When I touch a letter, you say the sound. Keep saying the sound as long as I touch it."
3.	Model new material	Show or tell students what they will learn	The teacher writes an i on the board. This letter is i. It represents the sound /i/. The teacher touches the letter and says the sound.
4.	Guided practice	Support students to perform the new skill correctly Provide immediate affirmative and corrective feedback	"When I touch the letter, you say the sound. Keep saying the sound as long as I touch it." Once students are accurate with the new sound, the teacher writes the i and previously learned letters on the board and says, "When I touch a letter, you say the sound. Keep saying the sound as long as I touch it."
5.	Independent practice	Move students from the accuracy phase to the fluency phase	Students practice touching the letters in a list and saying the corresponding sound.
6.	Apply the skill to new text or to a new problem	Application and generalization of the new skill	Students learn to blend the letter i with the letter t to read the word *it*.

Open Lessons Clearly

Each lesson should open with what students will learn and why it is important. Teachers should review prior skills and knowledge before introducing new content with unambiguous language and clear examples and nonexamples. Clear, direct models and language support novices to avoid confusion and to learn efficiently. Figure 2.2 (page 26) demonstrates a sample lesson opening.

> **Lesson Step 4:**
> **Phoneme-Grapheme Mapping, Teacher Model**
>
> "Because letters spell the sounds in words, I'm going to say the sounds in the word I want to write and then pull down letters to spell them. The first word is mit. The sounds are /m/ /i/ /t/. Watch me pull down the chips." (Put one chip in each box)
>
> The first sound in the word mit is /mmmmm/.
>
> Listen: /mmmmm/. I can use the letter m to spell the sound /mmmm/. I will put the m in the first box.
>
> The second sound in the word mit is /iiiii/. I can use the letter i to spell the sound /iiii/.
>
> The last sound in the word mit is /t/. I can use the letter t to spell the sound /t/. I will put the t in the last box.
> /mmmm/ /iiii/ /t/: mit.
>
> Watch me try another word."

Figure 2.2: Sample teacher language in a lesson opening.

> 1. Say the word.
> 2. Say each sound in the word.
> 3. Say the first sound in the word.
> 4. Write the letter that spells the first sound.
> 5. Say the middle sound in the word.
> 6. Write the letter that spells the middle sound.
> 7. Say the last sound in the word.
> 8. Write the letter that spells the last sound.

Figure 2.3: Breaking down the steps of writing CVC words.

Break Down Complex Information

Complex skills and strategies should be broken into smaller units of new material. Learning each component to mastery facilitates accurate and automatic performance of complex skills and strategies in students. This promotes carefully sequencing the teaching of skills as well as teaching the essential early literacy skills to mastery. Figure 2.3 is an example of what breaking down complex information might look like for the steps of writing consonant-vowel-consonant (CVC) words.

Sequence Content Purposefully

Content should be sequenced from easier to complex, with students mastering prerequisite skills before new skills are taught and teachers separating in time information that might be easily confused. Teaching in a purposeful sequence is efficient because it increases the likelihood that students will have the prerequisite knowledge needed to take on more challenging tasks. If the foundation isn't in place, teachers must backtrack and spend time reteaching. Figure 2.4 is an example of a purposeful scope and sequence for introducing sounds and letters over a period of thirteen weeks.

Promote Active Engagement

Instructors should deliver lessons at a brisk pace with attention to keeping students engaged and actively responding through choral responding, partner responding, and silent signals (table 2.3). Learning requires active processing of information (Willingham,

Weeks													
1	2	3	4	5	6	7	8	9	10	11	12	13
a, m	s, t	p, f	i, n	o, d	c, u	g, b	e, k	h, r	l, w	y, j	v, q	x, z

Figure 2.4: Sample scope and sequence for introducing sounds and letters.

2023). If students are not thinking, talking, or writing about the information, they are unlikely to transfer new learning from working memory to long-term memory so they can access it effortlessly in the future.

Table 2.3: Examples of Active Engagement

Engagement Strategy	Examples
Choral responding	Asking students to verbally respond in unison
Partner responding	Pairing students and alternating prompts for one partner to respond while the other listens, extends, or reacts
Silent signals	Teacher or students using gestures (such as hand signals like holding up a number of fingers, giving thumbs up or thumbs down, both hands in the air, and so on) that indicate an agreed-upon next step or response

Provide Feedback

Instructors should provide multiple opportunities for students to respond while monitoring performance and giving immediate affirmative and corrective feedback. Mistakes are the beginning and struggling reader's worst nightmare. Mistakes are hard to unlearn and increase the possibility of students not enjoying reading or disengaging with reading. In addition to reducing the possibility of making mistakes, teachers should structure instruction in a way that promotes many opportunities to check student learning. Teachers immediately acknowledge correct responses and immediately correct errors. In *Explicit Instruction: Effective and Efficient Teaching*, Anita Archer and Charles Hughes (2011) recommend a variety of active responses, which are detailed in table 2.4 (page 28).

Practice to Mastery

Students need to learn foundational reading skills such as vocabulary and word recognition not just for accuracy but all the way to mastery. Instructors can use the instructional hierarchy phases (accuracy, fluency, and generalization and transfer) to match students to the type of practice that will move new information into long-term memory. Table 2.5 (page 28) details the links between the instructional hierarchy phases and the different types of instruction and practice that best support students in each phase.

Prompted practice involves the use of scaffolds such as verbal reminders or visual supports. During *guided practice*, teachers closely watch students and offer immediate affirmative and corrective feedback. Independent practice works best after instructors observe consistent and accurate responses from students. *Cumulative and distributed practice* involves revisiting previously learned material over time.

Reading instruction has the potential to be more effective when it includes the elements of effective instruction this chapter describes. Some elements might be familiar to you, while others might seem foreign or even contrary to current instruction among your staff.

Table 2.4: Examples of Active Responding Based on Archer and Hughes (2011)

Choral Response	Partners	Written Responses
Teacher: Asks a question **Teacher:** Signals for response **Students:** Say answer together **Teacher:** Monitors responses **Teacher:** Provides feedback	**Teacher:** Asks a question **Teacher:** Gives think time **Teacher:** Designates partner one and two **Teacher:** Provides sentence starter **Student:** Shares answer **Teacher:** Calls on random students	**Teacher:** Gives clear directive **Students:** Write response **Teacher:** Circulates and monitors **Students:** Lower pencils to signal completion **Teacher:** Provides feedback to individuals **Teacher:** Provides feedback to group
Response Boards	**Hand Signals**	**Discussion**
Teacher: Gives clear directive **Students:** Write response on board **Teacher:** Circulates and monitors **Teacher:** Provides feedback to individuals **Teacher:** Asks students to hold up boards **Students:** Hold up boards **Teacher:** Monitors responses **Teacher:** Provides feedback to group	**Teacher:** Displays items on screen **Teacher:** Asks a question **Students:** Form number of fingers representing correct answer **Teacher:** Circulates and monitors **Teacher:** Asks students to hold up fingers **Students:** Hold up fingers **Teacher:** Provides feedback to group	**Teacher:** Introduces topic or asks question **Teacher:** Gives think time **Students:** Share with partner **Teacher:** Calls on random students **Students:** Share with class **Students:** Respond to classmates' ideas **Teacher:** Provides feedback
Echo Reading	**Choral Reading**	**Cloze Reading**
Teacher: Reads a word, phrase, or sentence **Students:** Echo read the word, phrase, or sentence	**Teacher:** Tells students, "Keep your voice with mine." **Teacher:** Reads selection orally at a moderate rate, modeling appropriate expression and rate **Students:** Read with teacher	**Teacher:** Reads orally **Teacher:** Deletes meaningful words and pauses expectantly **Students:** Read deleted word

Table 2.5: Linking the Instructional Hierarchy to Types of Instruction and Practice

Phase of Learning	Student Behavior	Type of Instruction or Practice
Accuracy	Slow and incorrect	More teaching Prompted and supported practice to increase accurate responding
Fluency	Slow and correct	More practice Guided and independent practice to build fluency
Generalization and transfer	Fluent and correct	More practice Cumulative and distributed practice for generalization

These principles of instruction apply to all students, not just students with disabilities such as dyslexia. It can be helpful to have a summary of the elements of effective instruction, such as the one in the "A.2: Elements of Explicit Instruction" activity (page 131).

The Leader's Role: Getting the Conditions Right

Ensuring all students read accurately, fluently, and for meaning is the fundamental responsibility of school leaders. The school leader's primary role in improving reading outcomes is getting the conditions right for teachers and interventionists to align instruction to research and student assessment data. You may not be the person delivering the instruction, but as the following Lead to Succeed case illustrates, you are the person who can set policy, purchase materials, allocate resources, organize professional learning, establish the schedule, and facilitate the use of data in collaborative decision-making teams. In future chapters, we will provide the details, processes, and materials for supporting that work.

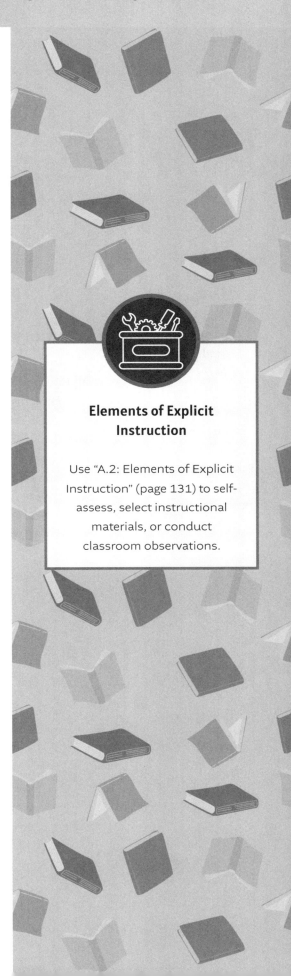

Elements of Explicit Instruction

Use "A.2: Elements of Explicit Instruction" (page 131) to self-assess, select instructional materials, or conduct classroom observations.

LEAD TO SUCCEED
Aligning Professional Learning

For years, your district has contracted with a consulting group to provide professional development and coaching to teachers. The consultants are well-respected and have established positive relationships with school and district staff.

Several teachers approached you after a recent workshop provided by the consulting group. The teachers expressed concerns about what they saw as a disconnect between the training provided by the consultants and their growing understanding of the research on effective reading instruction, as supported by training offered by the state office of education. The teachers' concerns seem nuanced and beyond your understanding of the research, so you add the topic to the next district leadership team meeting. In the meantime, it is important to grow knowledge of research on effective instruction and support teachers who are learning.

The school leader in this scenario validated the concerns of the teachers but was careful not to make quick decisions or try to go beyond the boundaries of their knowledge about the research on reading instruction.

Reflect and Connect

1. How are outside contractors evaluated for alignment to research and district goals?
2. How do you mediate disagreements about instructional practices?
3. What processes are in place for increasing alignment across various professional development providers?
4. Who can you trust when you need accurate information about reading research?

> When teachers know about the foundations of human learning, understand the elements of explicit instruction, and can match the needs of students to their instruction, the likelihood of student success increases.

Summary

Perhaps the most essential role of school leaders in reading improvement efforts is getting the conditions right for learning in each classroom. Simply knowing what to teach is not enough. The way instruction is designed and delivered is a critical component of student success. When teachers know about the foundations of human learning, understand the elements of explicit instruction, and can match the needs of students to their instruction, the likelihood of student success increases. Use the "A.1: Reading MTSS Reflection Guide" (page 126) to identify aspects of reading instruction to target for professional learning and coaching.

Ask Yourself...

- How do our teams determine reading tests to use?

- What reading tests are used throughout our district?

- How do we address gaps and duplications among the reading tests in our system?

- How do local building teams support teachers and families to understand why specific reading tests are used?

- How are reading data used to inform instruction?

CHAPTER 3
Navigating Reading Assessment

The right assessment guides instruction like a map guides a road trip. Assessment tells us where each student is currently and helps us determine what and how to teach so we have a specific route forward. It allows us to shift and adjust our instruction over time based on current outcomes. Local reading data inform that journey. And, because instruction is what leads to learning, it's essential to be smart about the amount of time spent on assessment. No educator wants to spend precious instructional time testing students, so ensuring that assessment time is targeted to get the answers to questions leaders and teachers have about student achievement is the best way to determine instructional next steps.

To get the most from the reading assessments that guide an MTSS, this chapter focuses on two main ideas. First, we explore the types of assessment needed to navigate reading instruction efficiently and effectively. We'll help you consider the use of your school's current assessments, as well as your school's unmet needs. Then, we explore ways to ensure that all teachers are engaged in your assessment plan. After all, if assessment is to guide instruction, educators need proactive support to understand how the data can support their reading instruction.

The Importance of Reading Assessment

When we fly on an airplane, we put our backpacks under the seat in front of us before takeoff. We may not even be exactly sure why we do it, but we know it's expected—and we're rule followers! In schools, we have become so accustomed to testing requirements that many times, we blindly administer tests throughout the year without thinking much about how the data will be used. These data have the potential to drive reading instruction to be more efficient and effective. There are three general principles of assessment that lay the foundation for reading assessment.

1. Assessment should be guided by questions.
2. Assessment should leverage indicators of reading proficiency in essential skills.
3. Assessment should use instructionally relevant tests.

Use Questions to Guide Assessment

We don't recommend responding to teachers' reading concerns by using a standard set of tests with each student. Instead, ask questions about students' skills and then assess toward answering those questions. For example, you may ask what phonics skills a student knows accurately. That specific question guides the assessment practices you use. At the system level, you may ask what percent of first graders meet middle-of-year screening targets to learn more about grade-level needs. By asking and answering educational questions, we end up with more actionable data.

Hopefully, it's clear that we view data as the source of answers to our questions. Without the foundation of educational questions, the resulting unspecific data are useless—a waste of time that could be spent teaching reading. If you don't have a specific question that an assessment will answer, then it doesn't make sense to use that assessment. That's one way that the problem solving that happens in the Collaborative Improvement Cycle (discussed in detail in the next chapter, page 47) supports assessment. It guides us through the types of questions to ask at various points in working with the system.

Leverage Indicators of Reading Proficiency

We started this chapter by recognizing that we need to minimize time in assessment to maximize instructional time. One way we do that is by assessing indicators. Indicators are data that are valid predictors of overall reading skills. When possible, it can be helpful to assess indicators of overall reading skills rather than taking time to directly test each individual reading skill. For instance, consider the simple view of reading we described in chapter 1 (page 11). We know that word recognition and language comprehension together work to create reading comprehension (Gough & Tunmer, 1986). Without knowing the research, many of us would assume that, to measure skilled reading effectively, we need to measure several skills within language comprehension and word recognition. But through research, we know that we can adequately predict skilled reading from a one-minute oral reading fluency measure (Hosp & Fuchs, 2005)—talk about maximizing instructional time! Oral reading fluency is an extremely strong indicator of overall reading skills.

You'll notice in table 3.1 that, in reading, many screening and progress-monitoring indicators are the same. Because these tests are very strong predictors of overall reading skills, they make logical sense to use as both screening and progress-monitoring tools. These measures have been shown to predict overall reading skills through replicated studies (Clemens, Lai, Burke, & Wu, 2017; Doty, Hixson, Decker, Reynolds, & Drevon, 2015; Fuchs, Fuchs, Hosp, & Jenkins, 2001). They can be quickly administered and can help building leadership teams identify system reading needs. And, because they are all either brief, one-minute measures or utilize existing data, they also can be used as progress-monitoring tools to measure student generalization of learned skills to overall reading skills.

Table 3.1: Tests That Serve as Overall Reading Indicators

Grade Level	Test and When to Implement
Kindergarten	Letter Naming Fluency (beginning of year)
	Letter Sound Fluency (middle and end of year)
Grade 1	Nonsense Word Fluency (beginning of year)
	Oral Reading Fluency (middle and end of year)
Grade 2–Grade 8	Oral Reading Fluency
Grade 9–Grade 12	State/provincial test proficiency

Implement Instructionally Relevant Tests

It can be difficult to focus assessments on questions about students when a school provides the same battery of tests (like IQ or general achievement tests) to use regardless of the reading concern. This is where instructionally relevant assessment comes into play. For example, a school psychologist could spend time measuring a student's IQ, but that test will likely not provide the information needed to help the teacher immediately in the classroom. We could measure a plethora of things that some may find interesting but that do not directly support classroom reading instruction. Like intelligence testing, skills such as processing speed (Rapid Automatized Naming—RAN) and visual-spatial reasoning do not directly inform evidence-based reading instruction (Kearns & Fuchs, 2013). Just because these skills are correlated with students' overall reading success, that doesn't mean they are useful to teachers or the best way to spend precious time in school. We can learn more about a student's reading needs with curriculum-based measures (CBM) that allow us to maximize instructional time by focusing on those skills that best support teachers to deliver targeted instruction.

Assessment Purposes in MTSS

As we've discussed, when we want to improve our instructional systems, we do so by asking questions and then searching for the answers to those questions. Assessment questions fall into specific purposes. When you know the purpose, you can best determine an assessment that will answer your question well. Table 3.2 (page 36) outlines the common purposes of assessment (Smartt, 2020; Torgesen, 2006). These purposes will be explored in greater detail later in this chapter.

Having a complete picture of the assessments your school or district currently uses and understanding the way those assessments support your MTSS in reading is a critical step. Use the team activities in this chapter (see appendix A, pages 133, 135, and 137) to identify assessment gaps and overlaps.

Grade-Level and Leadership Team Activities

Having a reading test map is a worthwhile way to document and drive data collection and review. This whole team activity occurs in phases.

First, grade-level teams complete the "A.3: Reading Tests Used" activity (page 133), documenting each of the tests used for the purposes described in this chapter by either some or all teachers.

Then, the building leadership team uses the "A.4: Building Reading Test Review" activity (page 135) to review the tests grade-level teams report using, adds any that are missing, and highlights those that are no longer on the district's testing plan.

Finally, the district leadership team uses the "A.5: District Reading Test Plan" activity (page 137) to review each building's testing plan and determine a districtwide strategy.

The building and district leadership teams can also review ideas and recommendations from grade-level teams to identify areas where teachers don't find value from current tests or aren't using them as you'd expect. These differences can guide professional learning planning on your assessment system.

Table 3.2: Purposes of Reading Assessment

Assessment Purpose	Description of Purpose	Connection to Reading Outcomes
Screening	Process of identifying student and system needs	Implement proactive and preventative reading supports so all students meet grade-level expectations
Diagnostic	Process of identifying specific skill gaps for students or groups	Match curriculum and instruction to student needs across all tiers
Progress monitoring	Process of evaluating student growth through frequent and regular assessment	Understand if the instructional package is effective
Outcome	Process of evaluating the results of instruction and intervention	Identify next system-level needs

Choosing Reading Tests

When you list the assessments you use and you reflect on how they support your MTSS in reading, many times you find either gaps or duplication. Some schools we work with find they have several tests being used to screen for reading skills but none that address specific questions about phonics they have. Others find they lack tools that are designed to be effective and efficient at monitoring students' progress over time.

Just because you have data from a test doesn't mean those data are adequate to answer the questions you have. The not-so-glamorous part of reading assessment is evaluating reading tests to ensure they give you the information needed to address your questions accurately. Each reading test educators use is designed and developed for a specific purpose. It's our job to ensure that we have tests that meet our needs *and* that we don't try to use tests to do jobs for which they aren't designed. The great news is that there are highly respected organizations that regularly review and summarize how well tests align with different purposes (National Center on Intensive Intervention, 2021). Educational leaders should feel confident asking questions about the reading tests they consider. Table 3.3 provides considerations leaders can use regarding the appropriateness of a reading test for their assessment purpose.

Table 3.3: Considerations for Choosing Reading Tests

Assessment Purpose	Key Considerations
Screening	<ul><li>Is it efficient to administer?</li><li>Does it have standardized administration?</li><li>Does it provide indicators of overall reading skills?</li><li>Is it predictive of reading proficiency?</li><li>Is it instructionally relevant?</li><li>Does is have documented reliability and validity?</li></ul>
Diagnostic	<ul><li>Does it directly measure key reading skills?</li><li>Does it provide multiple items for each reading skill, sequenced from easier to harder?</li><li>Does it have standardized administration?</li><li>Is it efficient to administer?</li><li>Is it instructionally relevant?</li><li>Depending on the use, does it have documented reliability and validity?</li></ul>
Progress monitoring	<ul><li>Is it efficient to administer?</li><li>Does it have standardized administration?</li><li>Does it provide an indicator of overall reading skills (demonstrated predictive validity)?</li><li>Is it instructionally relevant?</li><li>Is it sensitive to small skill improvements?</li></ul>
Outcome	<ul><li>Does it have standardized administration?</li><li>Are the outcomes sometimes high stakes (such as state/provincial tests)?</li><li>Are they administered at the end of a course or the end of the year?</li></ul>

Screening

Screening is the process of identifying student and system needs. Our focus, of course, is on the system. Leaders and teams must use screening data to reflect the effectiveness of instructional systems for all students. Screening must:

» Be efficient to administer

» Have standardized administration

» Have indicators of overall reading skills

» Be predictive of reading proficiency

» Be instructionally relevant

» Have documented reliability and validity

When districts consider reading assessments to use for screening purposes, the two most common types are Curriculum Based Measures (CBM) and Computer Adaptive Tests (CATs). Both types of tests have demonstrated technical adequacy for screening purposes.

CBMs serve as a General Outcome Measure (GOM), meaning they serve as an excellent indicator of skilled reading and measure the combination of language comprehension and word reading skills. CBMs are very brief (often one minute), the same for every student in a grade level, and always measure fluency.

CATs serve as a broad measure of a student's overall reading skills. They contain items that are aligned with standards. They are longer in nature (often fifteen to forty-five minutes) and vary the items based on student responses. Therefore, students do not receive the same assessment items and may be tested either above or below their current grade level.

Some CATs and CBMs have demonstrated reliability and validity that shows their appropriateness for making screening decisions (Clemens et al., 2015; Fuchs et al., 2001). Teams can be confident in using these data to answer questions about the overall effectiveness of reading instruction and intervention.

There is no one right way to collect system-level reading data. For screening in schools, a variety of methods have been used across time. In some schools, classroom teachers collect data, and in others, a small team collects data.

» **If you already collect data and use a small team to do so**, consider your teachers' collective efficacy around these tests. Answer this specific question: If you told them tomorrow that the test was going away, on a scale of 1 to 10, how hard would they protest to keep it? If the answer isn't an 8–10, then consider shifting to classroom teachers collecting some of the data themselves. The "A.6: Reasons We Assess" all-educator activity (page 139) may support discussions and consensus building around screening.

We aren't suggesting pulling the rug out from under teachers; rather, consider shifting practice a little. Train teachers to administer the test and then have them each choose three students—one they consider to be a high-performing reader, one average reader, and one reader who is at risk. They will administer the test to those three students. Then, after the testing window, meet immediately with grade-level teams to review their grade-level data but also what they noticed when they administered the test. This will give time to discuss any hesitations, questions, or concerns teachers may have about the test.

» **If you are going to begin administering a new test**, decide if either a small team and teachers will collect the data or if all teachers will collect the data themselves. It is important that even if teachers aren't collecting screening data for all students in their classroom, they're collecting it for some. Immediately after screening, schedule time to review their experience and the data. We are often quick to jump into the data (as we should be), but to build collective efficacy, we also need to take time to ensure that all teachers understand why we're using specific tests and how those data will help make their instruction more effective for their readers.

Diagnostic

The goal of collecting diagnostic data is to make a match to the specific skill and instructional needs of an individual or group of students. At the system level, the goal is to identify specific needs and plan class- or grade-level instruction and intervention. Used only when the information is needed to plan for instruction, diagnostic testing must:

» Directly measure key reading skills
» Provide multiple items for each reading skill, sequenced from easier to harder
» Have standardized administration
» Be efficient to administer
» Be instructionally relevant
» Depending on the use, have documented reliability and validity

Student-Level Diagnostic Assessment

Diagnostic information can be obtained from a variety of sources that do not require additional testing. For example, when students are identified as at-risk readers, information from screening data can be used by educators and specialists to make a first diagnostic match to local intervention resources.

As the students' skill deficits expand, or the stakes of a decision increase, the data collected need to be more rigorous in nature. Specific diagnostic tests should directly measure key reading skills and provide several assessment items for each reading skill assessed. Educators don't want to indicate that a student needs extra intervention on vowel teams, for instance, based on a single item assessing vowel teams. The diagnostic assessment needs to test each vowel team several times to lead teams to confidently plan an intervention on the skill.

And, as the stakes of the decision rise—for instance, if teams are considering removing learners from a portion of classroom reading instruction or labeling them as having a disability—the technical adequacy of the diagnostic measure also needs to be considered. In the case of diagnostic tests, they need to have *construct validity*, meaning they have been shown to measure the skill they claim to measure. This ensures that when we make these decisions, we can be confident we have the best instructional match to accelerate learning.

System-Level Diagnostic Assessment

At the classroom, grade, or school level, diagnostic assessment seeks to explain why a specific gap is occurring to support teams to address it in an intentional manner. For instance, a

Reasons We Assess

To help educators make the connection between assessment and instruction, facilitate a discussion during an all-educator meeting using "A6: Reasons We Assess" (page 139). Begin by sharing the results of your building's reading test plan, focusing on the connection between data and instruction. Have teachers discuss how the data purposes impact their instruction, as well as barriers they experience. Finally, ask educators to provide ideas for support they need to better use the reading data they collect.

This activity serves two purposes: (1) It gives educators an opportunity to learn and reflect on data use and how to improve the use of data to guide reading instruction, and (2) it also provides your building leadership team with valuable information to guide you in next steps of supporting teacher data use.

building leadership team may identify that the lack of protected reading instruction in the schedule every day is likely contributing to the high number of students who are not making expected reading growth. Teams can use a variety of data when conducting this *gap analysis*, or diagnostic assessment. Many times, information other than student reading data are supportive of these diagnostic efforts.

Types of Data to Support Gap Analysis

Diagnostic data to determine gaps in reading curriculum and instruction rely heavily on other types of assessment information besides tests. There are four types of data leaders can use to analyze system-level needs. Michelle K. Hosp, John L. Hosp, Kenneth W. Howell, and Randy Allison (2014) describe these four types of assessment data: (1) Testing is the type we most often refer to when we think of assessment, but we can also use (2) interview data, (3) review data, and (4) observations to gather information. Table 3.4 provides some examples of system questions each assessment type answers. While not an exhaustive list, it illustrates data sources that may provide direction to your team as you consider needs and next steps.

> At the classroom, grade, or school level, diagnostic assessment seeks to explain why a specific gap is occurring to support teams to address it in an intentional manner.

Table 3.4: Assessment Types and Reading Examples

Type of Assessment	Example Question	Example Data
Review	• Are we able to complete one lesson in each session in reading intervention? • Are we able to complete the entire first-grade curriculum program by the end of the year?	• Curricular materials, such as lesson completion within curriculum materials
Interview	• What is our level of self-efficacy with using our curricular materials? • How effectively are we able to use MTSS to drive instructional decisions at the grade level? • What should we focus on within an MTSS for our professional learning next year?	• General education teachers regarding their confidence with evidence-based reading instruction, use of the curricular materials, or knowledge about MTSS • MTSS implementation self-assessment
Observation	• How effectively are teachers using elements of explicit and systematic instruction? • How effectively are teachers using a specific instructional routine we expect to be used?	• General education reading lesson
Test	• Which students are at risk of not being successful readers? • Do we need to intensify our reading instruction? • How effective are our interventions at improving reading achievement?	• Universal screening • Progress monitoring • State/provincial assessment

Educators often rely on testing data because it's the information that comes to mind first and is often most readily available. However, using a variety of sources of reading data can often lead to a more complete picture of student skill needs and easily identify the best next step. The Lead to Succeed case that follows is an example.

LEAD TO SUCCEED
Considering Various Types of Data

After middle-of-year universal screening data in reading were collected, your building leadership team reviewed the information and noticed that beginning- to middle-of-year reading growth was not meeting the expected targets at both first and fourth grades. During the discussion, team members shared a variety of reasons growth may have been lower, including questioning the quality of the reading screening assessment, the ambitious nature of the growth goal, and the need for more reading interventionists at those grade levels.

After the meeting concluded, you realized that the only information considered were those student data and decided to go talk to the first- and fourth-grade teams during their team meetings. During those interviews, you discovered that the fourth-grade team had not used the research-based curricular materials for about a month because they decided to read a novel. And, in reviewing the curricular materials with the first-grade team, you learned they decided to skip the practice on previous skills embedded in each lesson.

With this additional information, you head back to the next leadership team meeting with data that can best help the team make a more informed decision regarding next steps.

—

The team member in this scenario did a great job by considering the other types of information that may result in the best next steps. When we make evidence-based decisions, our course of action hinges on the data available to us. Having only student data often leaves us without enough information about the broader context that resulted in those data. Continuing to ask questions and explore the reasons for the data can make it easier to learn the right actions to take to improve reading outcomes.

—

Reflect and Connect
1. When making decisions about system needs, what types of data do you currently consider?
2. How do you expect the data you review impacts the recommendations and next steps you take?
3. How might you expand the options of information to collect and review when considering system changes?
4. What are ways you may introduce teams to the various types of data you may consider when making system-level reading decisions?

Progress Monitoring

Progress monitoring is the frequent and repeated measurement of student skills, with a valid and reliable tool, to measure the effectiveness of instruction and intervention. As with screening, districts and teachers have choices related to choosing progress-monitoring tools. In reading, we recommend measuring an indicator (such as oral reading fluency, for example) because it will ensure the skills being taught through intervention are supporting students to progress toward grade-level proficiency. The same indicators in table 3.1 (page 35) are the CBMs that should be used as a default progress monitoring tool for students receiving intervention and special education services at respective grades. Progress-monitoring tools must:

» Be efficient to administer

» Have standardized administration

» Include indicators of overall reading skills (demonstrated predictive validity)

» Be instructionally relevant

» Be sensitive to small skill improvements

These tests are very strong predictors of overall reading skills; therefore, they make logical sense to use as progress-monitoring tools. They can be quickly administered, which is essential for ensuring they are used frequently and regularly. The results can also be aggregated to support grade-level and building leadership teams to identify reading intervention system needs, a concept we will explore further in chapter 7 (page 97).

Remember, instruction doesn't necessarily need to focus solely on the same skills assessed. When third-grade students are receiving intervention focused on phonics skills, for example, oral reading fluency is likely still the most efficient and effective measure of progress toward how those students' instruction and intervention supports them to make progress toward overall reading skills.

Outcome

Outcome assessment provides a summary of student learning. Districts and schools use it to identify program-level needs as well as for reporting individual student learning, such as in report cards. Outcome assessment is also valuable for the purposes of program evaluation and identifying system needs. For example, if a high school building leadership team notices that 28 percent of freshman fail the Geometry I end-of-course test, meaning they did not meet geometry standards, the team may prioritize support for those students and educators the following year. Outcome assessments often have the following characteristics.

» Have standardized administration

» Typically, be high stakes (such as state/provincial tests)

» Often administered at the end of a course or unit

Schools must note that while these tests are helpful for summarizing the learning of individual students, they are much more helpful as system-level information. Because they occur after learning has occurred, as opposed to during instruction, outcome assessments are not as useful as screening, diagnostic, and progress monitoring assessments at guiding individual student instruction. They do provide important information for systems that seek to identify grade levels or programs that may need additional improvement to meet the needs of students.

Summary

Reading assessment can guide instruction, but there are also many complexities and barriers that must be considered when choosing and implementing reading tests. Leaders must consider the purpose of their assessments, how their tests align with their MTSS framework, and ensure they are designed to be used to answer the questions their system asks. Finally, leaders must support educators to best be able to collect and understand how the data are used for them to impact student reading success. Use the "A.1: Reading MTSS Reflection Guide" (page 126) to consider next steps for building an impactful reading assessment system.

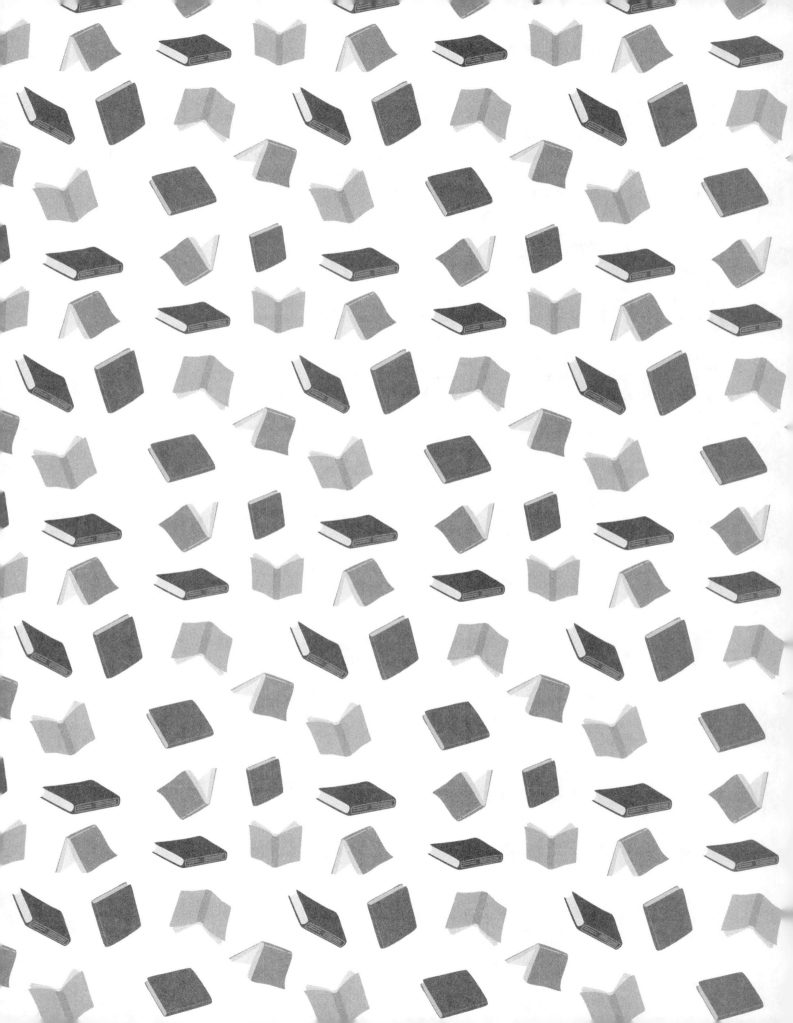

PART II

Engineering a Robust System of Support

Ask Yourself...

- Which teams are working to improve reading outcomes in our school? Are the right people on those teams?

- Which assessments are used by individuals and teams for improving reading outcomes?

- How do teams at all levels of the system use a decision-making framework to design, implement, and evaluate tiered reading instruction?

- How are student reading data used to make decisions about professional learning and coaching?

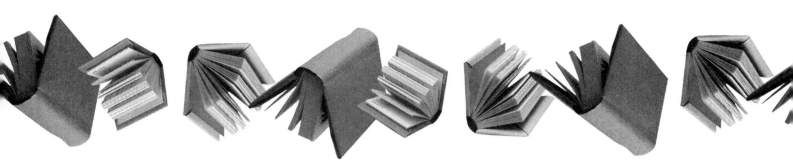

CHAPTER 4
Foundations of MTSS

The core beliefs that underlie the MTSS model include the following (Jimerson, Burns, & VanDerHeyden 2016; McIntosh & Goodman, 2016; Simmons et al., 2000; Sugai & Horner, 2006).

- » All children can learn—if they haven't learned it, we haven't taught it the right way for them to learn it.
- » Students are learning in schools, which are complex host environments.
- » All educators should make decisions through shared ownership and leadership.
- » Evidence should guide decisions.
- » Outcomes are prioritized over ideology and beliefs.

This chapter describes the problems that led to the creation of what is now called MTSS and why it is the ideal framework for implementing what is in the reading research. MTSS directs the way data are used to engineer a system of increasingly intensive instructional supports that meet the needs of all students. MTSS is an approach to ongoing school improvement that contextualizes the reading research to match the resources and challenges of your staff, students, and community.

The Origins of MTSS

As you learned in the first few chapters, much is known about how reading develops, what can go wrong, and how to prevent and intervene when students have reading difficulties. One of the key findings of the reading research is that most reading problems can be prevented through the way reading is taught in kindergarten and first grade (Torgesen, 2002). The goal of using student data to build systems of prevention and intervention, what we now call MTSS, has been the focus of education change efforts for many decades.

MTSS originated in the late 1980s in reaction to unintended negative outcomes of the 1975 passing of The Education of All Handicapped Children Act (PL 94–142), which

> One of the key findings of the reading research is that most reading problems can be prevented through the way reading is taught in kindergarten and first grade (Torgesen, 2002).

required districts to find and serve students with disabilities. It was a true triumph that students with disabilities were now educated in public schools, but this seismic shift in service delivery was not implemented without glitches. The 1982 report of the National Academy of Sciences (Heller, Holtzman, & Messick, 1982) called into question the value of categorical service delivery for all students with disabilities in general, and it highlighted the specific issue of overrepresentation of minority students. The 1986 document Rights Without Labels was developed and endorsed by several national associations to advocate for students with disabilities to be given specially designed instruction without requiring a label or removal from the general education classroom. At about the same time, the Office of Special Education and Rehabilitative Services at the United States Department of Education released *Educating Students With Learning Problems: A Shared Responsibility* (Will, 1986). The report called for elimination of the dual systems of general and special education and the formation of a unified system that supports all teachers to be effective with all students. In 1989, the National Association of School Psychologists released an edited text called *Alternative Educational Delivery Systems: Enhancing Instructional Options for All Students* (Graden, Zins, & Curtis, 1988).

Three of the main concerns with educational service delivery identified in the 1980s that still persist today are (1) separate general and special education systems, (2) students have to fail before getting help, and (3) using the wrong kinds of assessments. These concerns form the basis for planning and systems change within the MTSS model for reading improvement.

Separate General and Special Education Systems

Shortly after creating the special education system of support for students with disabilities, educators realized that silos had been established that became a barrier to getting students the support they needed. Teachers who worked with students with disabilities were given separate titles and separate training both in college and once they were on the job. Special education was funded by different federal and state dollars and governed by a different set of laws, policies, and procedures. A system for administering special education was established in districts and state offices of education, separate from the existing systems for administering general education programs, without much communication between the two. These actions created parallel systems that rarely communicated or interacted for the benefit of students.

Students Have to Fail Before Getting Help

Because special education funding, personnel, and policies were separate and different from general education, rigid barriers were built that made it difficult for a student to "get into" special education. Unfortunately, the entry criteria tended to focus on how far behind a student was from their peers. Initial attempts to reasonably allocate special education services resulted in a pre-referral system called Intervention Assistance Teams (IATs). The goal of IATs was for teams of educators to use student data in a decision-making framework (such as the Data-Based Problem Solving Model; Deno, 1989) to resolve student concerns with low-intensity resources in general education to reduce the number of students who needed intensive, special education resources. Sadly, many IATs became nothing but a set of hoops for educators to jump through on the path to special education eligibility, with the result being reinforcement of the wait-to-fail approach.

The Wrong Kinds of Assessment

In the 1980s, when serving students with disabilities in public schools was relatively new, there was heavy emphasis on the "specialness" of students who received special education. School psychologists and diagnosticians received training in expensive and opaque individual assessments of students that perpetuated the beliefs that the "problem" was within the student rather than the instructional environment, emphasized categorizing and labeling students, and promoted an expert model in which decisions about eligibility for special education were made almost entirely without connection to classroom reading performance.

Beyond Student-Level Problem Solving

In the late 1990s and early 2000s, reports by the National Research Council and National Reading Panel synthesized the research findings on how children learn to read. The federal grant program called Reading First provided a mechanism for developing schoolwide models of reading support that built on the ongoing alternative service delivery models and newer work in behavioral support (Walker et al., 1996). Some states built upon the integrated service delivery movement to create three-tiered models of academic and behavioral support (Batsche et al., 2006; Ervin, Schaughency, Goodman, McGlinchey, & Matthews, 2006; Graden, Stollar, & Poth, 2007). By 2004, the federal laws governing special and compensatory education included the phrase *response to intervention* (RTI). Unfortunately, this led to many districts focusing on using data-based decision making only to resolve student-level concerns. More recent efforts to shift to the term MTSS are an effort to return to the use of data-based decision making to resolve system-level barriers to student success that were originally identified in the 1980s (Jimerson et al., 2016).

Resolving these issues and barriers forms the basis of the MTSS model of reading improvement that is the focus of this book. Without addressing the systemic issues that make it difficult to meet the literacy needs of every student, the use of the three-tiered model in MTSS will continue to be just another set of hoops to jump through on the path to special education, resulting in overwhelmed staff and underserved students. Successful implementation of tiered supports that benefit all students depends on integrating aspects of the school system to support reading improvement. The system levers for change are described in the next section.

MTSS System Levers for Change

The essential elements of MTSS are the five levers for system change that school leaders and other educators can use to improve reading outcomes.

1. An impactful assessment system
2. Effective and equitable tiered supports
3. Targeted professional learning
4. Strategic leadership and teaming
5. Collaborative improvement cycle

These levers represent deliberate attempts to move away from the flaws with the previous service delivery model to one that is more flexible, integrated, and focused on meeting students' needs with the least intensive resources possible. Some educators still equate MTSS with RTI, with a narrow focus on moving students through three tiers on the way to special education. In our image of MTSS, shown in figure 4.1, at the base of the tiers we depict the system levers that distinguish MTSS from other school improvement approaches. These are the aspects of a school system that leaders must consider in order for the tiers to function for students. The tiered model itself contains all resources in the school. The "A.1: Reading MTSS Reflection Guide" (page 126) provides a tool for teams to self-assess the current use of these system levers for change. In this way, MTSS can become the overall framework for all reading improvement efforts (implementing dyslexia laws, the science of reading, PBIS, and so on) thus avoiding random acts of improvement.

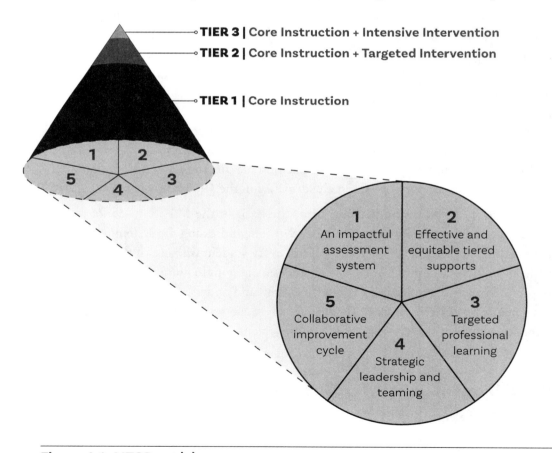

Figure 4.1: MTSS model.

Impactful Assessment System

Efforts to improve reading outcomes begin with clear and accurate data on current student performance. Implementing the MTSS model for reading improvement requires having a system of coordinated assessments for four purposes: (1) screening, (2) diagnostics, (3) progress monitoring, and (4) outcome evaluation. As discussed in chapter 3 (page 33), having these sources of data on students allows educators to contextualize the reading research to the needs of their students and build a system of support for all learners.

Effective and Equitable Tiered Supports

The tiered system of instruction and intervention is based on research about prevention and early intervention. Most reading problems can be prevented (Torgesen, 2002). Prevention is easier and more effective to implement in schools than intervention. Intervention is resource intensive and not as likely to be effective. Therefore, it is important to prevent reading difficulties in kindergarten and first grade, provide intervention early in every grade, and use classroom reading instruction to reduce the number of students who need intervention. Table 4.1 (page 52) describes the key features of each tier.

An effective MTSS for reading requires a coordinated system of instruction within and across tiers. The tiers contain various school resources that provide support. One component of a tiered system is the materials that are used, often in the form of published programs. The elements of effective reading instruction should be apparent in programs used across tiers. Now that you know what research says about the design and delivery of reading instruction, you can evaluate the instructional approaches and programs your school and district use. Selection and use of programs used as part of tiered systems should be matched to local student needs.

The MTSS model relies on three types of research-aligned programs: (1) core, (2) supplemental, and (3) intervention.

1. **Core:** Core reading programs are comprehensive materials used to teach initial and differentiated instruction in the regular classroom. Core reading programs provide the content and instructional priorities (the curriculum), as well as the sequence, materials, and delivery method that cause students to meet the grade-level standards. They should result in equitable growth and equitable outcomes across student groups.

2. **Supplemental:** Supplemental reading programs can be used in Tier 1 or 2 when the Tier 1 reading program doesn't provide enough instruction or practice in key areas to meet local student needs. They can be used with all students to supplement the Tier 1 reading program, or as intervention in Tier 2 to provide extra support to ensure students meet grade-level standards.

3. **Intervention:** Intervention programs provide well-designed, high-quality instruction for students who are not proficient in reading. They are typically used with some students receiving Tiers 2 and 3 resources (as an addition

Table 4.1: Tiers of Support

	Tier 1	Tier 2	Tier 3
Purpose	Primary prevention of reading failure	Secondary prevention of reading failure	Tertiary prevention of reading failure
Program Type	Core and supplemental programs	Supplemental and intervention programs	Intervention
Effectiveness	At least 80 percent of students meet grade-level expectations through Tier 1 instruction alone	An additional 15–20 percent of students reach expectations with Tiers 1 and 2.	The remaining 5 percent of students reach expectations with Tiers 1 and 3.
Characteristics	High-quality, equitable general education reading instruction • Provided by the classroom teacher or other educators such as special educators, paraprofessionals, reading specialists, coaches, speech and language pathologists, and other personnel determined by school resources • Instructional methods and materials based in effective instruction and culturally responsive practices • Minimum of ninety minutes each day • All students • Whole-group and small-group formats	Strategic reading instruction using research-aligned, culturally responsive programs and methods • Provided by the classroom teacher or other educators such as special educators, paraprofessionals, reading specialists, coaches, speech and language pathologists, and other personnel determined by school resources • In addition to, not instead of, Tier 1 instruction • Approximately thirty to forty-five minutes three to five times per week • Students who are at risk for reading difficulties despite receiving generally effective core reading instruction • Small, flexible, skill-based groups of three to five students	Intensive reading instruction for individualized, research-aligned, culturally responsive support • Provided by the classroom teacher or other educators such as special educators, paraprofessionals, reading specialists, coaches, speech and language pathologists, and other personnel determined by school resources • In addition to, not instead of, Tier 1 instruction • Approximately forty-five to sixty minutes daily, and individualized as needed • Students with identified reading concerns as determined by screening, diagnostic, and progress-monitoring data • Small, flexible, skill-based groups of one to three students
Relationship to Collaborative Improvement Cycle	Team: • Grade level • Building level Assessment tools: • Universal screening three times per year • Diagnostic assessment	Team: • Grade level • Building level Assessment tools: • Universal screening three times per year • Progress monitoring at least every other week (often weekly) • Diagnostic assessment	Team: • Student level • Building level Assessment tools: • Universal screening three times per year • Progress monitoring weekly • Diagnostic assessment

to Tier 1 reading instruction). The purpose of intervention programs is to accelerate learning and close gaps.

It is not necessary to have different programs for each tier of support. In fact, using different programs within the school day is not only overwhelming to beginning and struggling readers, but it is potentially counterproductive because, many times, these different programs follow separate scopes and sequences of skills. For example, working memory is taxed when students are taught vowel teams in one time of the day and letter–sound relationships in another. Additional confusion can occur when different terms are used for the same skill, like the CVCe pattern (vowel consonant E; magic E; silent E). Instructional time is lost when students have to think about the correct way to respond in one setting versus another or when they are unsure about the next step in the routine.

It can be helpful to see aspects of an MTSS in comparison to current practices. Clearly defining and describing the tiered model and how those systems of support are implemented in your school is an important first step. The "A.7: Our Programs" activity (page 140) supports school leaders to discuss current practices in relationship to the MTSS model.

The following Lead to Succeed example illustrates the importance of aligning instruction across tiers. Although it can be difficult to realize that your initial reading improvement efforts have not had the desired impact on student outcomes, it is important to remain open to ongoing revision and continuous improvement.

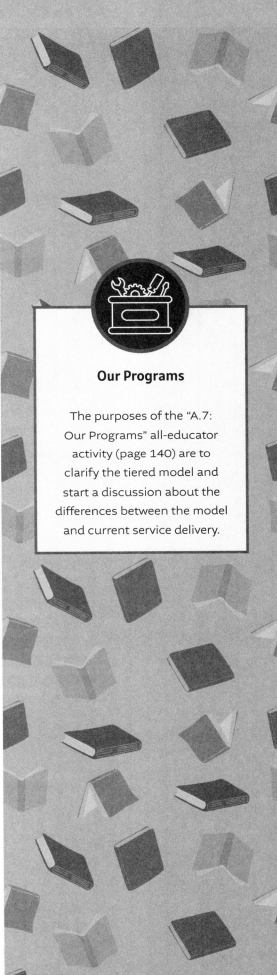

Our Programs

The purposes of the "A.7: Our Programs" all-educator activity (page 140) are to clarify the tiered model and start a discussion about the differences between the model and current service delivery.

LEAD TO SUCCEED
Aligning Across Tiers

Your third-grade team reviewed data after the end-of-year screening and noticed that the percentage of students on track with reading comprehension had declined across the year. Students who started the year on track stayed on track, but students who started the year behind were not catching up. You decide to dig in more deeply, and through reading a research article and consulting with your special education staff, realize that students with Individualized Education Programs (IEPs) are spending time in instruction that is too difficult for them. Based on this information, your team decides to align the instruction used in Tier 1 and Tier 3 to the needs of the students.

Given this rather significant change, there are several things the building leadership team can do in this scenario to align instruction across tiers.

- Share the research article with all staff and hold an optional after-school session to discuss what they learned and why they made the decision.

- Write a special newsletter to teachers and parents explaining the decision, why they made it, and emphasizing the goal of prioritizing improving reading outcomes over previous ways of operating.

- Each grade-level team representative on the building leadership team uses the same information and materials to discuss the decisions in a grade-level team meeting. The principal and special educators join each of those meetings to reinforce support for the decision and to tackle any uncomfortable conversations that arise.

- Provide training and coaching to all staff to promote effective implementation of the instructional routines.

Effective teams don't need to do all these things, but aligning instruction across tiers can help build systemic implementation of new practices.

Reflect and Connect

1. What opportunities exist for reflecting on the effectiveness of current programs and materials?

2. Which staff members have deep knowledge of reading research and can access journal articles?

3. How are decisions made about purchasing, evaluating, and de-implementing instructional materials?

Clarity is essential for novice and struggling readers. Think about students' daily school experiences by considering the following questions.

» Do all programs use the same scope and sequence?

» Do they use teacher language and terminology in the same way?

» Do they use the same instructional routines?

» Is it necessary to use different programs across the tiers or can the same effective program be intensified?

School leaders can increase the likelihood of adopting effective programs that meet the needs of their students by thoughtfully assembling a representative team of stakeholders (such as district and school leaders, teachers, paraprofessionals, special educators, related service personnel, and parents and community members) and providing them with the time and tools to make recommendations. The place to start is with student data.

Universal screening and diagnostic data at each grade level can help answer questions such as the following.

» What is the level of literacy skill at kindergarten entry? At the start of each grade?

» What do assessment results indicate about the type of grouping format that should be used?

» Which skills should be taught in whole group versus small groups?

» Are the student needs the same in the primary and intermediate grades?

Many published programs, especially core reading programs, aim at pleasing everyone by including multiple approaches to reading instruction, even if they are not aligned to research. It would be impossible to implement everything in these programs in a typical school day or school year. When considering adopting new materials, reviewers should focus on unpacking the guts of the instructional scope and sequence, routines, and practice opportunities. Tools like the *Consumer's Guide to Evaluating a Core Reading Program* (Simmons & Kame'enui, 2003) and The Reading League's *Curriculum Evaluation Guidelines* (2023) provide a starting place for reviewing the extent to which research-aligned elements of reading instruction are evident in programs under consideration. Objective tools also help to guard against the tendency toward the familiar and the influence of enthusiastic salespeople. The "A.8: Reading Instruction and Intervention Program Audit" (page 142) tool helps teams see the programs used for instruction and intervention at each grade so they can fill gaps and align across tiers.

Having the right programs is only part of the equation. Teachers need adequate time in the daily schedule to implement the adopted programs and time to plan with colleagues. They also need expertise to intensify materials to meet students' needs.

Every school leader knows the challenges involved with creating the school schedule. While it would be impossible for this book to address the specific details of each school schedule, here are some general guidelines.

» Prioritize achieving the optimal schedule in kindergarten and first grade to prevent reading failure by the end of first grade.

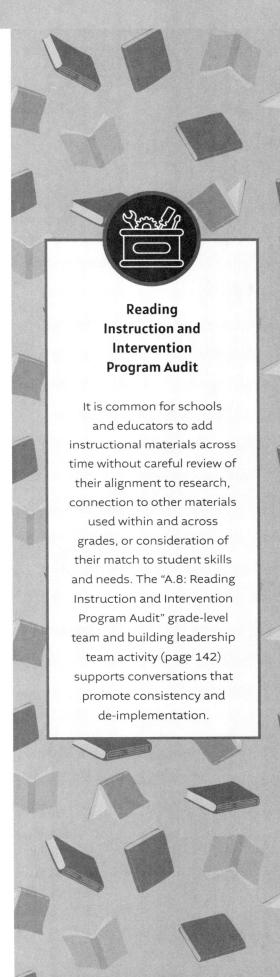

Reading Instruction and Intervention Program Audit

It is common for schools and educators to add instructional materials across time without careful review of their alignment to research, connection to other materials used within and across grades, or consideration of their match to student skills and needs. The "A.8: Reading Instruction and Intervention Program Audit" grade-level team and building leadership team activity (page 142) supports conversations that promote consistency and de-implementation.

- » Use the percentage of students who score below expectation to inform the length of time scheduled for Tiers 1 and 2 (more struggling students may mean more instructional minutes) and how the time during Tier 1 will be used.
- » Stagger the time when Tier 1 is taught across the grades to allow all adults to flood the grade. Available adults will vary across systems but could include special educators, English learner staff, remedial reading staff, and paraprofessionals.
- » Schedule all adults who support a grade level to have common planning time at least monthly.
- » Proactively engage the teachers' union and parents in any possible changes to the schedule.
- » Think flexibly about how adult resources are allocated so you move beyond rigid barriers imposed by titles, funding streams, or past practices.

Scheduling Time to Plan Instruction

At least once a week, teachers and others who support the grade level should meet to review data and plan changes to Tier 1 and Tier 2 instruction. In a future chapter, you will learn how to use student data in the Collaborative Improvement Cycle model. This is where student assessment data, information about the instructional hierarchy, and the elements of effective instruction will come together to benefit all students.

Scheduling Time to Deliver Instruction

Tables 4.2 and 4.3 are two sample schedules for a school with a high proportion of struggling readers. Table 4.2 illustrates a daily timetable for kindergarten to third grade, and table 4.3 shows time allocation in first-grade Tier 1. Notice on the daily schedule how the times for Tier 1 and Tier 2 instruction are staggered across the grades to allow support staff to flood each grade during Tier 1 and provide additional support at another time of day during Tier 2 and 3 intervention. Notice on the Tier 1 schedule how decisions about grouping format were made based on student needs.

Similarly, table 4.4 depicts a sample middle school schedule with eight instructional periods, including two electives. Again, notice staggered intervention periods. This would allow for cross-grade grouping, if needed, based on student skills. During intervention periods, schools may choose a variety of other activities. Some schools may allow students to participate in additional elective courses, others will have structured study periods, while others will offer intervention for all, with additional practice or extension opportunities for students who are on-track in reading.

Targeted Professional Learning

You may have concluded that moving your system toward more effective reading instruction is likely to involve changing or expanding your colleagues' knowledge, beliefs, and instructional practices. When some school leaders first learn about the science of reading, they sometimes make the mistake of immediately purchasing new programs, only to later

Table 4.2: Sample Elementary Daily Schedule

	K	1	2	3
8–9	Tier 1	Tier 1		
9–10				
10–11			Tier 1	
11–12				Tier 1
12–1				
1–2	Grade-level planning	Grade-level planning	Grade-level planning	Grade-level planning
2–3	Tier 2		Tier 2	
3–4		Tier 2		Tier 2

Table 4.3: Sample First-Grade Tier 1 Schedule

Time	Format	Skills
Seventy-five minutes	Whole group	Vocabulary
		Syntax
		Listening comprehension
		Content knowledge
		Writing
Forty-five minutes	Small group	Phonemic awareness
		Phonics / spelling
		Reading fluency
		Reading comprehension

Table 4.4: Sample Secondary Daily Schedule

	6	7	8
8:30–9:00	Homeroom	Homeroom	Homeroom
9:03–9:43	Core class	Core class	Core class
9:46–10:26	Intervention	Core class	Core class
10:29–11:09	Core class	Core class	Intervention
11:12–11:52	Lunch	Core class	Elective
11:55–12:35	Core class	Elective	Lunch
12:38–1:18	Elective	Lunch	Intervention
1:21–2:01	Core class	Intervention	Elective
2:04–2:44	Intervention	Elective	Core class
2:47–3:27	Elective	Intervention	Core class

regret the purchase when they are more knowledgeable about reading research and the needs of their students. This puts leaders in the awkward position of having to retract previous program adoptions and mandates. Leaders can avoid this by building the knowledge of the staff and school community first, before purchasing new materials and programs. Successful teams use their understanding of the research and avoid relying on websites or asking nearby districts what they use.

Once new programs are adopted, school leaders must ensure adequate time is allocated for training and coaching on the programs. A helpful approach might be to take a three-year perspective, supporting staff to learn and use the new program in the first year, differentiate its use in the second year, and improve upon it in the third year. School leaders and others can support implementation by using the elements of effective reading instruction when they observe classroom instruction and provide ongoing, job-embedded coaching of program use and its alignment with evidence-based reading curriculum and instruction.

> When some school leaders first learn about the science of reading, they sometimes make the mistake of immediately purchasing new programs, only to later regret the purchase when they are more knowledgeable about reading research and the needs of their students.

Strategic Leadership and Teaming

School leaders play a vital role in implementing MTSS for reading improvement. Someone must keep everyone moving in the same direction when the going gets tough! Leaders have the role of removing barriers to implementing reading instruction within an MTSS and work with their supervisor and peers to keep the building focused on reading improvement. Whether you have the word *leader* in your title or job description or not, you can embrace the essential role of guiding colleagues to do whatever it takes to get every student reading.

The daily and ongoing work of MTSS happens in teams at all levels of the educational system. While every team uses the Collaborative Improvement Cycle, the focus and membership of each team are different. We explore team membership and functions in chapter 5 (page 65).

The Collaborative Improvement Cycle

In the MTSS model for reading improvement, teams of stakeholders use assessment data in a structured problem-solving model to remove barriers at the student, grade, school, and district levels. At the core of the MTSS model is the use of the Collaborative Improvement Cycle to resolve barriers to reading achievement. The Collaborative Improvement Cycle is based on using a structured process of identifying, analyzing, and resolving student concerns referred to as *data-based decision making* (Deno, 2016; Filderman, Toste, Didion, Peng, & Clemens, 2018; Fuchs, Fuchs, Hamlett, & Stecker, 2021) and *collaborative problem solving* (Batsche et al., 2006; Deno, 1989; McIntosh & Goodman, 2016), and resolving systems concerns under the term *collaborative strategic planning* (Curtis & Stollar, 2002). We chose to use the Collaborative Improvement Cycle to reflect the ongoing nature of reading improvement work and to emphasize the prevention of, not just the solving of, problems facing schools. The term *collaborative* refers to the manner in which teams of stakeholders use data to make decisions. While individual educators can also use The Collaborative Improvement Cycle to resolve issues, there is power in working together to resolve common barriers to success. The word *improvement* reminds us that the goal is to improve reading outcomes. The term *cycle* indicates the ongoing nature of this work. Figure 4.2 depicts the cyclical nature of the steps.

> At the core of the MTSS model is the use of the Collaborative Improvement Cycle to resolve barriers to reading achievement.

The Collaborative Improvement Cycle is used by all teams at all levels of the educational system to identify and eliminate district-, school-, grade-, and student-level barriers to student success. Table 4.5 outlines the basic steps of the Collaborative Improvement Cycle.

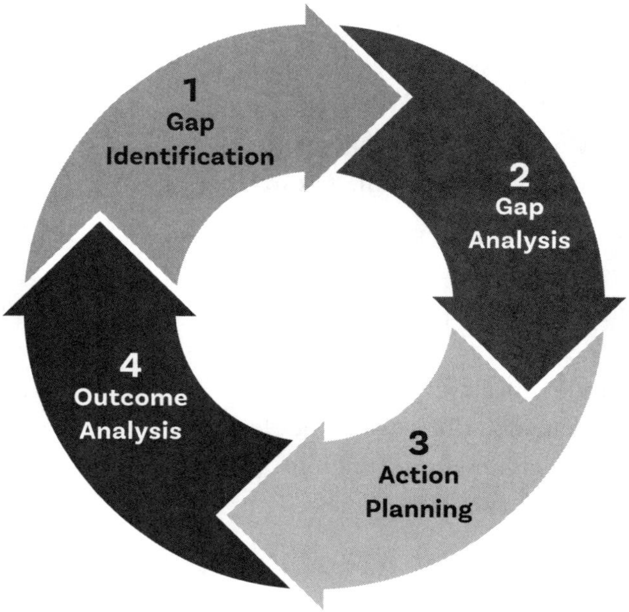

Figure 4.2: The Collaborative Improvement Cycle.

Table 4.5: Steps of the Collaborative Improvement Cycle

	Step	Question	Description
1	Gap identification	What is the gap between actual and desired outcomes? Which systems and students need support?	Teams should define the gap as precisely as possible; it is the difference between what is expected and what is actually happening in the system.
2	Gap analysis	Why is the gap happening?	Teams should consider student, instruction, and environment variables, barriers, and resources to generate hypotheses about the factors contributing to the gap.
3	Action plan	What is the plan?	Teams use information from step two to create a plan. This includes setting a goal, identifying necessary resources, and stating how progress will be monitored.
4	Outcome analysis	Is the plan working? Did the plan work?	Student and implementation data are used to determine if the plan needs to be revised. Teams may return to step one or two if reading growth is inadequate.

Rather than being a linear process, as the table suggests, the Collaborative Improvement Cycle is a recursive, self-correcting process that is grounded in the belief that if students aren't learning, the adults in the system haven't yet implemented the right conditions for learning. Some models of reading improvement may focus assessment and problem analysis on variables that are internal to the student. We find these approaches to be limiting and prefer to view the student as a learner within multiple overlapping systems that involve community, district, school, and classroom variables, as depicted in figure 4.3, all of which provide opportunities for change that can improve results.

Use of Collaborative Improvement Cycle and the Connection to the Science of Reading

Many schools have implemented team planning to resolve academic or behavioral concerns about individual students. These meetings go by a variety of names—teacher-based teams, intervention assistance teams, case study teams, and even (inaccurately) as professional learning communities (PLCs). For reference, figure 4.4 (page 60)

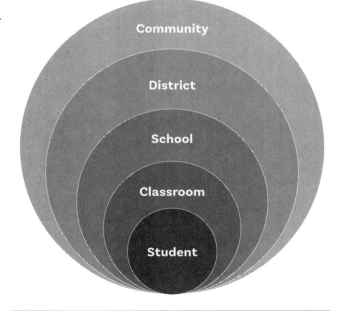

Figure 4.3: Students learn to read within multiple interrelated systems.

shows an example of the Collaborative Improvement Cycle process applied to an individual student concern. The problem is that most schools have too many students who are at-risk or struggling readers. These student-level teams get bogged down and don't produce intervention plans that can be sufficiently resourced and implemented, which results in no real change in student reading outcomes.

Step	Question	Example
1. Gap identification	What is the gap between desired and actual performance?	At the beginning of third grade, students should read grade-level text accurately, fluently, and for meaning. John meets expectations for reading accurately but not fluently or for meaning.
2. Gap analysis	How and why is the gap happening?	Hypothesis: John is an accurate reader but not fluent in grade-level text. His low reading comprehension is caused by lack of fluency.
3. Action plan	What should we do about it?	Engage in repeated reading of text to build fluency.
4. Outcome analysis	Is it working?	At the middle of the year, John met expectations for accuracy, fluency, and comprehension.

Figure 4.4: Collaborative Improvement Cycle applied to student concern.

The MTSS model applies planning and the Collaborative Improvement Cycle to the educational system to reduce the number of students for whom student-level planning is necessary. We believe that this system-level work is missing from most reading improvement laws, policies, and implementations.

Specifically, two key components of MTSS are missing from many reading improvement efforts.

1. Using aggregate student data as an indicator of instruction and intervention effectiveness

2. Team-based planning for intervening on the system barriers to student achievement

In the MTSS model, teams initially focus on getting the learning conditions right for all students by analyzing and improving classroom reading instruction, thus reducing the number of students for whom individual student planning is needed. For example, teams look at the percentage of students in each grade who have or don't have essential literacy skills. If a large proportion of incoming kindergarten students lack initial phonemic awareness skills, classroom instruction is designed to meet this need rather than removing those students from classroom instruction to receive intervention. The use of aggregate data to analyze instruction and intervention effectiveness and systematically remove barriers to students' achievement is the work of district, school, and grade-level teams.

At all levels of the educational system, MTSS involves teams using data in the Collaborative Improvement Cycle to build a tiered system of evidence-aligned instruction to meet the needs of all students. Learning to use collaborative teaming time in this manner requires training and ongoing coaching. Over time, this approach to resolving issues and implementing change can support all members of the school community to use the Collaborative Improvement Cycle to resolve any issue that comes their way. Table 4.6 shows an example of using the process to resolve a system-level concern.

> The MTSS model applies planning and the Collaborative Improvement Cycle to the educational system to reduce the number of students for whom student-level planning is necessary.

Table 4.6: Example of the Collaborative Improvement Cycle Used by District, School, and Grade-Level Teams

Step	Question	Example
1. Gap identification	What is the gap between desired and actual performance?	At the beginning of third grade, 100 percent of students should read text accurately, fluently, and for meaning, but only 50 percent of our students meet these expectations.
2. Gap analysis	Why is the gap happening?	Forty percent of the students in this grade can't read basic CVC but all phonics instruction is provided in whole groups.
3. Action plan	What should we do about it?	Provide explicit and systematic phonics instruction in Tier 1 and Tiers 2 or 3.
4. Outcome analysis	Is it working?	All steps of our action plan were implemented. Seventy-five percent of students now meet grade-level expectations on middle-of-the-year screening.

An essential finding of reading research that is operationalized in MTSS is prevention of reading difficulties (Simmons et al., 2000; Snow, Burns, & Griffin, 1998; Torgesen, 1998, 2002). When the percentage of students who meet grade-level expectations isn't increasing across the school year, school leaders and their teams should first consider the way reading is taught in Tier 1, regular classroom reading instruction. If universal reading instruction was improved, fewer students would need interventions, and resources would be available for those who need intensive intervention. In contrast, when there is only a small proportion of students who are receiving interventions, and they are not catching up to grade-level expectations, school leaders and their teams should first consider the way reading is taught in Tier 2 and Tier 3 supports.

Many educators are familiar with using a data-based decision-making framework such as the Collaborative Improvement Cycle to address student-level concerns. The problem is that this process is time and resource intensive. When teachers are asked to work through this process with several students in their class, they quickly become overwhelmed and frustrated. Schools with many struggling readers are unlikely to have the capacity to work through the process with every student who is struggling. The unfortunate result is that some students go to the next grade without the reading intervention they deserve. The alternative offered in the MTSS model of reading improvement is to apply the Collaborative Improvement Cycle to system-level concerns, primarily to reduce the number of students for whom the intensive individual Collaborative Improvement Cycle process needs to be conducted. Additional support to do this will be provided in chapters 6 and 7 (page 81 and 97).

Summary

Collaborating to use data for reading improvement is a complex and challenging job. But it is the work that must be done in response to the reading crisis. When teams use the Collaborative Improvement Cycle to address system needs related to reading teaching and learning, teams avoid common struggles with putting system-level data to use to drive reading improvement. The "A.1: Reading MTSS Reflection Guide" (page 126) can guide use of the Collaborative Improvement Cycle to create reading action plans.

Ask Yourself...

- How do district and building teams eliminate barriers to improve reading outcomes?

- How are important stakeholder groups and experts represented on district and building teams?

- How do teams communicate with each other?

- How do teams document their plans and hold themselves accountable to implementing their improvement efforts?

- How might we use teaming and collaboration to support collective efficacy amongst educators in our setting?

CHAPTER 5
Teaming to Support Reading Improvement

Teaching can be a lonely job; the education profession has always been one in which its members are prone to working independently. Teachers are in their classrooms for most of the day, with little time for teaming and often no time to observe other instruction in action. This experience leads educators to be unlikely to share their teaching successes and failures with each other and, thus, results in inequity in instructional quality and student growth from classroom to classroom. As educators, we all hope to be in a school someday where every teacher's classroom is one in which we can guarantee exceptional reading growth. A collaborative culture with strong collective efficacy is a key to this future.

This chapter is focused on supporting the work of reading improvement using existing teams, clarifying the work of those teams, or creating new teams. First, we outline the teams that typically do the work in MTSS. Next, we specify the roles and functions of those teams. Then, we emphasize the importance of communication within and across teams. Finally, we support the use of decision making by teams at all levels.

> As educators, we all hope to be in a school someday where every teacher's classroom is one in which we can guarantee exceptional reading growth.

The Importance of Teams in Enacting Reading Change

Teams serve an essential role in supporting reading improvement efforts through an MTSS (Helman & Rosheim, 2016). While educators are engaging in learning about reading science, teams support the acquisition of new knowledge and skills. As they advance in their ability to teach and differentiate reading expertise, teams support educators to generalize and adapt their skills to meet a variety of students' needs. Teams are critical to educator collaboration, collective efficacy, and the ability to solve tough educational problems (DuFour et al., 2024).

Collaboration

Most educators value collaboration and wish they had more time to work closely with other teachers. Working collaboratively can accelerate the rate of change in complex organizations like schools. We are, in fact, better together (Johnston, Knight, & Miller,

2007). Collaborative organizations put action to the belief in the value of all viewpoints, accomplish goals more quickly, and avoid dissent and sabotage by including all voices in planning from the start. Moving forward into uncharted waters is easier when you know your coworkers are with you, rowing in the same direction.

Collective Efficacy

Related to collaboration is collective efficacy. *Collective efficacy* refers to the belief that we can achieve our goals by working together, using each team member's strengths and perspective (Bandura, 1993; Donohoo, Hattie, & Eells, 2018). Teams with high collective efficacy are incredibly important to the task of improving reading outcomes because they are more likely to share their wins (and losses) with each other. This sharing not only builds the collective knowledge of the team but also provides the opportunity to reflect on how our actions contribute to learners' reading achievement and growth. This increases not only the team's effectiveness but also increases overall shared leadership and capacity for implementing change. When we think we can, we do.

Collaborative Improvement Cycle

Using a structured decision-making process makes our collaboration actionable, efficient, and effective. The Collaborative Improvement Cycle gives structure and purpose to the aspirations of partnership, inclusion, and viewpoint diversity—we are coming together for the purpose of solving real problems facing our students, school staff, and community. When all members of the school community learn to approach problems and use data in the same way, team meetings are focused and efficient (Ruby, Crosby-Cooper, & Vanderwood, 2011).

In chapter 4 (page 47), we explored the Collaborative Improvement Cycle process that permeates MTSS. This chapter focuses on the groups that use that process to remove barriers and get the conditions right for reading success.

Teams and Their Functions

There are a plethora of teams in schools. To support driving reading improvement through an MTSS, some team functions are essential. In a perfect world, you will already have have the types of teams we have mentioned and can align some of their conversations with your reading improvement priorities. If that's not the case, we recommend doing an inventory of current teams, using the "A.9: Our Teams" tool (page 143) to document current teams and details about their work to allow you to repurpose and retire teams, as appropriate. An example of a completed version of this tool appears in figure 5.1 (page 68).

As you consider the teams we discuss, focus on the roles, responsibilities, and purposes of each team, as opposed to considering if your current teaming structure needs to match ours. We do not ever recommend just adding these teams to the existing teams in your school; that would be certain to overwhelm educators and overburden schedules. Effective MTSS implementation depends on the right people getting together to use the

Collaborative Improvement Cycle to write implementation plans that involve identifying resources that can be used to eliminate barriers to better reading outcomes.

Types of Teams

Teams at each level of the school system, including at the district, building, grade, and student levels, serve different purposes and make different decisions. They sometimes use similar data, but often also use different data to support their decision making.

» **District- and building-leadership teams** use adult implementation data (information on the extent to which we were able to take the action we planned) and aggregate student data to get a big-picture view of the effectiveness of the instruction and intervention systems in each school. This is the system-level work that is the focus of this book. Because this teamwork is focused on system-level issues, the teams' role is to prioritize improvements, proactively support change, and analyze and remove the barriers to improving outcomes for large groups of students. They make decisions about policy, staffing, professional learning, schedules, materials, and more.

» **Grade-level teams** also work at the system level. They collect and use screening and progress monitoring data and use them to inform the implementation of the instruction (Tier 1) and intervention systems (Tiers 2 and 3) at their specific grade level. Depending on the district, they may make decisions regarding schedules, grouping, materials, and specific interventions. Grade-level teams may use screening and diagnostic data to design and implement intervention systems at Tiers 2 and 3. These teams then collect and review progress-monitoring and adult implementation data for each intervention group to determine needed next steps for the group. The needs of individual students or groups of students may be discussed related to Tier 1 instruction, but individual student intervention is usually not the focus of this team. Small schools with only one section per grade won't have grade-level teams and those functions will be performed by the building leadership team.

Our Teams

The "A.9: Our Teams" leadership team activity (page 143) allows you to see a landscape of current teams in your district or building and evaluate gaps and redundancies. You may be able to start filling in the inventory yourself, but we recommend sharing it with those on teams to see if they agree or would adjust some of your thoughts about what teams are responsible for and how often they meet.

Team	Purpose	Topics	Members	Meeting Frequency
District	Use aggregate data to identify and remove barriers to better reading outcomes. Write a district reading improvement plan.	Policy Hiring Professional learning Instructional materials	Superintendent Central office administrators Building administrators Representatives from teaching staff, related services, and the community	Monthly
Building	Inform and implement a building improvement plan aligned with the district improvement plan. Write a building reading improvement plan.	School-level data Professional learning Instructional materials Staffing Schedule Community engagement and communication	Building administrator Representatives from each grade, related services, and the community	Every other week
Grade level	Inform and implement the building reading improvement plan	Grade-level data Professional learning and coaching Instructional materials Staffing Schedule Family communication	Teachers Special educators All staff who serve students in the grade	Weekly
Student	Write an individual reading improvement plan	Instruction and intervention Student data	School administrator Teacher Relevant related service personnel Parents and community members	As needed

How do teams communicate with each other?
At quarterly planning meetings, with email between chairs, and via shared meeting minutes

How do teams communicate with the district office?
Via members of the district leadership team and email to the district leadership team chairperson

How do teams communicate with caretakers?
Email, monthly newsletter, and community forums

Figure 5.1: Sample Our Teams completed activity.

> » **Student-level teams** use individual student screening, diagnostic, and progress monitoring data, as well as adult implementation data, to design and implement intervention for students who are receiving more intensive and individualized reading support. These teams use more individual data about a student's skills and past instruction and intervention to determine the best instructional package for the student moving forward. This is one of the only teams where membership tends to be fluid, determined by the individual students they are serving. Caregivers and community partners should be members of their child's student-level teams.

Team Membership

Improving reading outcomes requires all members of the school community to work toward the same goals and contribute to the successful implementation of improved reading programs. For each team, leaders can use the purpose and decisions that the team makes to identify the appropriate stakeholder groups. The unique perspective of each of these groups truly leads to better decisions and plans.

For instance, consider a building leadership team whose function is to make decisions, support implementation, and remove barriers to high-quality instruction for all students in the building. It is important for the building administrators to be represented as they likely are key to each of those functions. Also, if every grade level may be impacted by decisions made by the team, each grade level will need a representative. If decisions are being made about reading in particular, a reading content expert needs to be on the team, along with a representative who can advocate for learners with unique needs impacted by these decisions, such as a special education or multilingual learner representative. A parent may also be a useful team member to support caregiver engagement. Although they are not serving as an advocate for their own child, they will provide a critical perspective to decisions and planning.

While every educator has a voice, is fully informed of what is changing about reading instruction, and understands why those changes are necessary, not every educator needs to be on a team. We recommend each critical stakeholder group have a representative on the team and that work is done to ensure each team member understands their role as the representative of another group. One way to evaluate if current teams have the right stakeholders who participate is to do a team review during an all-staff meeting.

Communication

When team membership is as we describe in the previous section, not every educator is a part of every team and every decision. For example, the school psychologist may be a member of the building leadership team as a representative of the related services staff (speech-language pathologist, occupational therapist, physical therapist, social worker, and counselor), or a parent may be a member of the district leadership team as a representative of family members in the district, not as an advocate for their own child.

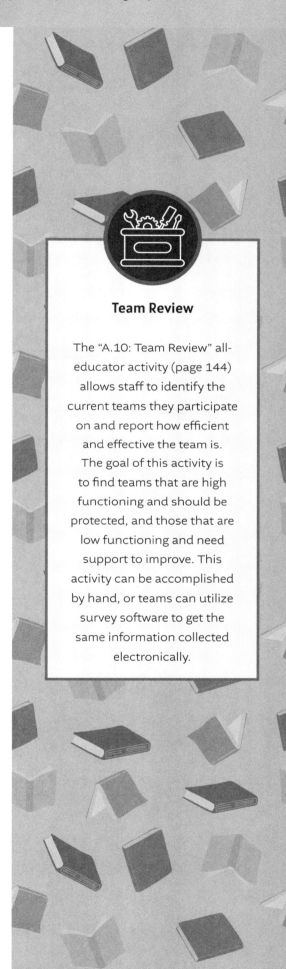

Team Review

The "A.10: Team Review" all-educator activity (page 144) allows staff to identify the current teams they participate on and report how efficient and effective the team is. The goal of this activity is to find teams that are high functioning and should be protected, and those that are low functioning and need support to improve. This activity can be accomplished by hand, or teams can utilize survey software to get the same information collected electronically.

In this case, making change requires planning for two-way communication between teams and ensuring that representatives are trusted members of the stakeholder group they represent. There are several ways to support this two-way communication.

One of the most helpful ways to gain consensus from all educators for decisions and changes from district and building leadership teams is to ensure that everyone has similar background knowledge. Thus, when making a change, considering how to share information about the what, why, and how of the decision is critical.

Most educators agree with this concept, but in practice, it can be challenging to implement. We recommend setting up supports to make it impossible to forget to consider these essential two-way interactions. Meeting agendas are a great way to get this structure. When a common meeting agenda always includes a section on communication, teams are more likely to discuss and decide what stakeholders need to know.

The same structure can be used when preparing for a meeting, as well. When sending out the meeting agenda, the facilitator can include questions to gather input from each stakeholder group to ensure that everyone's voice is in the conversation. Not every topic needs that level of input, but ones in which controversial or complex decisions are being made can benefit from these practices. The Lead to Succeed case that follows is an example of a schoolwide change and the communication plan that followed.

> Thus, when making a change, considering how to share information about the what, why, and how of the decision is critical.

LEAD TO SUCCEED
Effective Communication

Your building leadership team reviewed data at the end of the school year and noticed that they were no longer using the running records data that had been collected for many, many years. You decide to dig in more deeply, and through reading a research article and consulting with your school psychologist, realize that your new universal screening tool in reading provides more technically valid data and is more efficient to administer, saving valuable reading instructional time. Based on this information, your team decides to stop using the running records assessments for the next school year.

—

Given this rather large change, there are several things the building leadership team can do to help build consensus for this new practice.

- Share the research article with all staff and hold an optional after-school session to discuss what they learned and why the decision was made.

- Write a special newsletter to teachers explaining the decision, why it was made, and how they feel confident that everyone will have the important information needed to successfully plan instruction.

- Each grade-level team representative on the building leadership team uses the same information and materials to discuss the decisions in a grade-level team meeting. The principal joins each of those meetings to reinforce support for the decision and to tackle any uncomfortable conversations that arise.

- After universal screening at the beginning of the next school year, reading experts (coaches or interventionists) join each grade-level team meeting to ensure that all educators feel confident to interpret and use the newer universal screening data, and that they are comfortable explaining those data to caregivers.

Effective teams don't need to do all these things, but supporting two-way conversations when significant change is implemented can help build consensus, and thus, systemic implementation of new practices.

—

Reflect and Connect

1. What opportunities exist for reflecting on current practices?
2. Which staff members have deep knowledge of reading research and can access journal articles?
3. What processes do you have in place for building consensus?
4. How are you creating consistency and coherence by communicating across teams?
5. How do you ensure that all stakeholders provide input on and receive updates on key decisions?

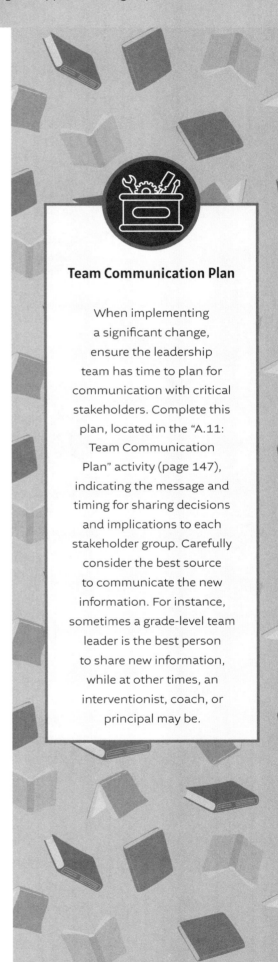

Team Communication Plan

When implementing a significant change, ensure the leadership team has time to plan for communication with critical stakeholders. Complete this plan, located in the "A.11: Team Communication Plan" activity (page 147), indicating the message and timing for sharing decisions and implications to each stakeholder group. Carefully consider the best source to communicate the new information. For instance, sometimes a grade-level team leader is the best person to share new information, while at other times, an interventionist, coach, or principal may be.

When substantial changes are made to reading practices, impacting a variety of stakeholders, like caregivers and educators at multiple grade levels, a separate communication template may be useful. Consider the "A.11: Team Communication Plan" (page 147) in these situations. For instance, if a new reading curriculum is being implemented in K–5, there may be several items that need communication related to training, coaching, materials, and things that will be replaced by these new curricular materials. It can be helpful to spend time in a team meeting planning for communication around each of these items. See an example of a completed Team Communication Plan in figure 5.2 (page 72).

Meeting Facilitation

Most educators would say they lack enough time to collaborate with their colleagues. And, when we have time to collaborate,

Level of Urgency	Key Information to Communicate	Audience	Person Responsible	Frequency
This information is: • Nice to know • Need to know • ⟨Need to act⟩	Meeting minutes	District Leadership Team All staff Parents and community	Team note taker	After every meeting
This information is: • Nice to know • Need to know • ⟨Need to act⟩	Action steps	People involved in the actions	Chairperson	After every meeting
This information is: • Nice to know • ⟨Need to know⟩ • Need to act	Agenda items for next meeting	Members of building leadership team	Grade-level team representative	Before every meeting
This information is: • Nice to know • Need to know • Need to act				

Figure 5.2: Sample completed Team Communication Plan.

working together in an effective and efficient manner does not necessarily come naturally, nor is it always easy. Conversations about how to intensify reading instruction, change student groupings, and collect additional data can be difficult, especially when educator perspectives and expertise are different. MTSS team meetings are not informal discussions and thus benefit from specific protocols and guidance for addressing confusion or hurdles when they arise. We recommend using training, meeting roles, and meeting agendas to support effective and efficient meetings within an MTSS framework.

» **Training:** Team facilitators often benefit from specific training to support their group-facilitation skills to ensure that they are listening to the team and are confident in keeping the meetings focused and on track. This training often focuses on both the content that is discussed in meetings and strategies to engage all participants, ensuring all voices are heard, and managing challenging conversations.

» **Meeting roles:** Another way to support team facilitators is to end each meeting by deciding on roles for the next meeting. When the facilitator isn't also responsible for ensuring the meeting is running according to agenda times and documenting decisions and notes, they can tune in when there's a team member who isn't participating as much as they normally do or focus on guiding the team through a challenging decision. An added bonus of having roles in meetings is that it builds shared leadership, collective efficacy, and ownership over the decisions the teams make.

» **Meeting agendas:** We find that meetings implementing an MTSS framework to address specific reading needs benefit from agendas that serve as meeting protocols. These guide teams through the specific questions they need to answer at a given meeting and point them to the data that will support their decisions. Common meeting agendas also ensure that meetings are efficient. There are some data or reports that teams only review once or twice a year. It's easy to forget about a specific report or remember a decision that needs to be made when it's infrequent, so having those reminders in an agenda can be helpful.

When external coaching for facilitators and effective teaming isn't available, team members can lean on agendas and guidance from each other in leading effective meetings to improve reading instruction and outcomes.

We believe in supporting facilitators to lead effective meetings so much that the third part of this book consists of meeting protocols leaders and teams can use throughout a school year to support teams to meet all students' needs in reading.

Collaborative Improvement Cycle to Support Teams

When used as part of team meetings, the Collaborative Improvement Cycle approach, described in chapter 4 (page 47), provides teams at all levels with a structured, organized, and thoughtful process of asking questions and using data to support students and educators. Teams ask similar questions at meetings for both the system level and the student level. Use of the Collaborative Improvement Cycle differentiates MTSS from other reading improvement approaches with the structure of asking questions and using data to proactively respond to student and educator needs. Use the "A.12: Teams and the Collaborative Improvement Cycle" activity (page 148) to review teams that use the Collaborative Improvement Cycle. Figure 5.3 (page 74) provides a sample Collaborative Improvement Cycle describing a school's teams.

Common Teaming Challenges and Solutions

Finding Time to Team

Many schools have MTSS teams that meet regularly to explore and address student-specific concerns. Adding to their purpose the system-level work described in this book will obviously come

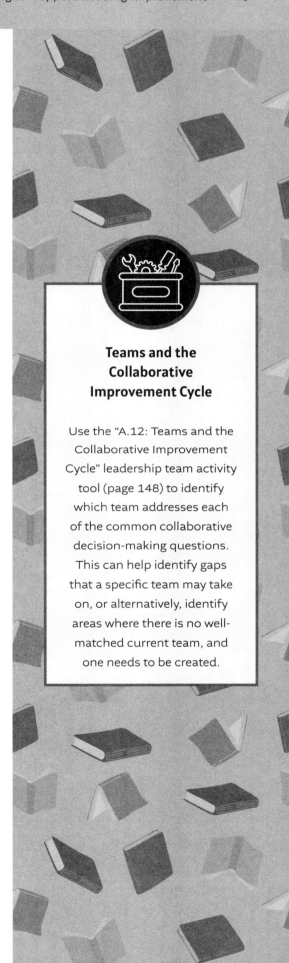

Teams and the Collaborative Improvement Cycle

Use the "A.12: Teams and the Collaborative Improvement Cycle" leadership team activity tool (page 148) to identify which team addresses each of the common collaborative decision-making questions. This can help identify gaps that a specific team may take on, or alternatively, identify areas where there is no well-matched current team, and one needs to be created.

For each of the following activities that teams engage in related to system-level reading improvement, identify your local team that is appropriate for this responsibility.

Levers for System Change	Do we have a local team that currently addresses this? If so, which team?	If not, is there a current team that is a correct match to address this? If so, which team?	Action Needed
Team structures and membership	District leadership team		~~No action needed~~ Communicate with team Create team
Designing, implementing, and evaluating Tier 1	Building leadership team Grade-level teams	Review grade-level team Tier 1 responsibilities at the next building leadership team meeting.	No action needed ~~Communicate with team~~ Create team
Designing, implementing, and evaluating Tier 2	Grade-level teams		~~No action needed~~ Communicate with team Create team
Designing, implementing, and evaluating Tier 3	Grade-level teams		~~No action needed~~ Communicate with team Create team
Assessment tool selection	District leadership team		~~No action needed~~ Communicate with team Create team
Assessment data collection	Building leadership team		~~No action needed~~ Communicate with team Create team
Assessment data usage	Grade-level, building, and student teams		~~No action needed~~ Communicate with team Create team
Training and coaching on how to use Collaborative Improvement Cycle	District, building, and grade-level teams		~~No action needed~~ Communicate with team Create team
Training and coaching on assessment system	District, building, and grade-level teams		~~No action needed~~ Communicate with team Create team
Training and coaching on science of reading	District, building, and grade-level teams		~~No action needed~~ Communicate with team Create team

Figure 5.3: Sample teams and Collaborative Improvement Cycle activity.

with scheduling considerations. Schools we work with have taken different approaches to making time to have system-level discussions and implement the Collaborative Improvement Cycle. Some discover that current teams aren't functioning consistently across grade levels and buildings and find that resources like professional learning, agendas, and data protocols make current time more focused and effective. For teams that need additional time, schools may use rotating substitutes to allow for team planning time during the school year at critical periods (such as immediately after beginning-of-the-year screening) and provide stipends for work in the summer to engage in larger system improvement efforts.

There are many ways to create time for this collaborative work, and it doesn't all involve adding more meetings to teachers' already-full calendars.

Resistance to Using Data Regularly to Drive Instruction

Educators don't necessarily default to using data to make decisions. It makes sense, as they often haven't had support to analyze and act on those data alongside their colleagues. School leaders are responsible for creating a culture in which having and using data is supported and expected. This involves listening to educator feedback and their conversations during meetings and then reflecting about the current system, including where the system itself is creating unintentional barriers to using data to improve reading outcomes through MTSS. There are some actionable ways to proactively plan for team consensus and address resistance to MTSS you may experience.

1. Provide ongoing training and support to all educators on how to use assessment data to inform instruction.

2. Schedule monthly meetings for instructional leaders, coaches, or other experts to meet with each teacher to review the progress of students in their class and small groups.

3. Provide data protocols and agendas that rely on data at each meeting where instructional changes are discussed (such as student problem-solving meetings, IEP team meetings, and so on). Avoid making high-stakes decisions (such as referral for a special education evaluation or writing an IEP) without progress-monitoring data. We've worked in schools where if a progress-monitoring graph isn't present, the meeting is canceled and rescheduled.

4. Model the use of data-based decisions during staff meetings, showing how you've used data in the other decisions you're communicating with educators. Include agenda items on those meetings to discuss the actions being taken in response to the percentage of students who are on track in each grade and their outcomes. Taking time not to just celebrate growth but to call out the actions educators have taken to achieve that growth builds collective teacher efficacy.

5. Provide ongoing staff professional learning on how to connect test scores to the implementation of the core reading program and reading interventions.

6. Regularly communicate student outcomes to stakeholders such as central office staff, the superintendent, and the school board. This can include reporting on an increase in the percentage of students who are on track or describing how teachers changed instruction and student outcomes improved.

7. Streamline testing requirements and de-implement overlapping tests to make time for educators to collect and use direct, curriculum-based screening and progress-monitoring data. This also maximizes instructional time.

8. Require and support teachers to confidently share student progress monitoring data with families and caregivers during conferences. Support them with discussion outlines and perhaps even practice with colleagues.

9. Support family members to discuss data with their child's teacher. Include a description of the universal screening tool, what it is used for, and how it helps educators support learning in the school handbook or on a parent-accessible website.

10. Communicate about student data in school newsletters and other electronic communications. Talk about student reading growth, as well as what educators are doing to support that growth, in each grade at family and community events such as open house and family literacy nights.

By strategically supporting and expecting regular data use, we find educators embrace, and see value in, a culture of using data to drive instructional decisions.

Summary

Teams provide the environment in which to build capacity, empower educators to grow collective efficacy, and ensure important perspectives are included in key decisions. Thoughtful consideration of team membership, team purposes, communication within and across teams, and meeting facilitation, as guided by the "A.1: Reading MTSS Reflection Guide" (page 126), may make a large difference in your ability to move the needle on reading success using an MTSS framework.

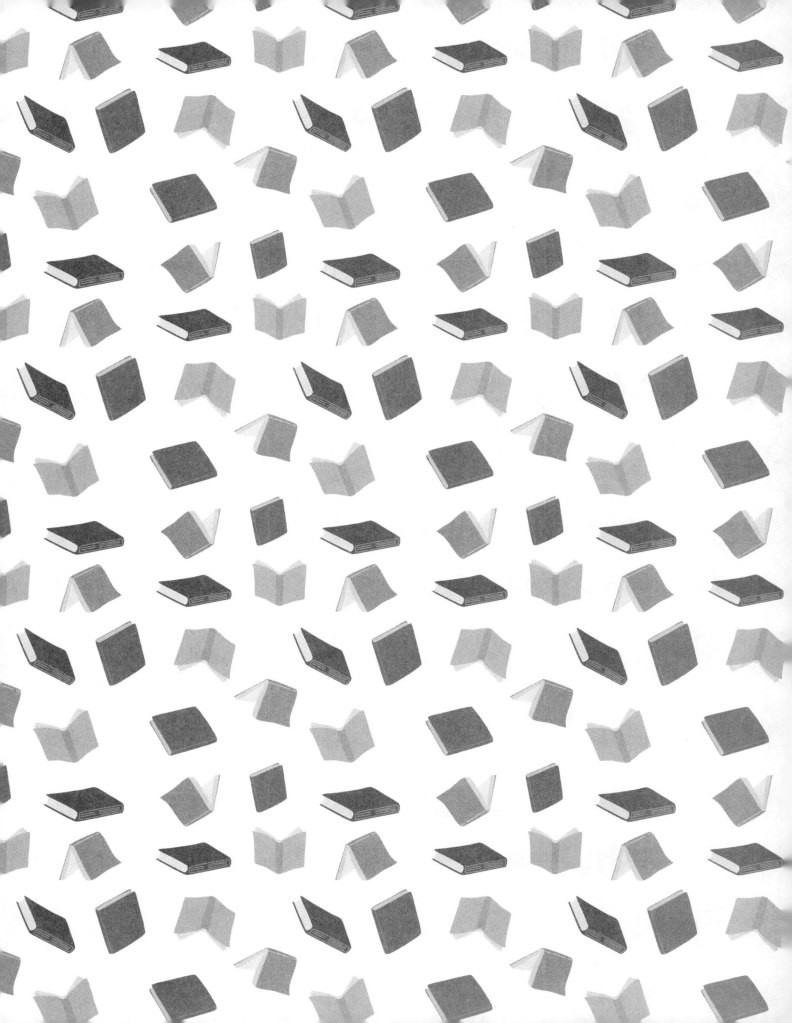

PART III

Enabling Educators to Improve Reading Outcomes

Ask Yourself...

- How are teachers currently supported to implement and improve their Tier 1 instruction? What about new teachers?

- What opportunities exist for teams to use screening data to answer system-level questions about the effectiveness of Tier 1?

- How are teams supported to use screening data to analyze and improve Tier 1?

- What concerns do we expect local stakeholders to have about analyzing and addressing Tier 1 needs? How might we address those concerns?

CHAPTER 6
Using Data to Drive Tier 1 Reading Instruction for All Students

Lawn and landscaping practices vary based on where you live. The trees, bushes, and flowers you plant are influenced by common principles applied to your specific climate, such as water availability and temperature. For instance, Sarah divides her time between the Midwest and Southwest, and her landscaping is adapted to each region. In the Midwest, based on water availability, she has a grassy lawn, while in the Southwest, her yard consists of rocks. Both homes have a variety of trees, bushes, and plants that are chosen based on water, sunlight, and temperature in that region.

The same is true for Tier 1 reading instruction in schools. Rather than seeing the science of reading as a singular program or collection of rigid changes, each school and district must adapt the reading research to their specific needs, resources, and challenges. The principles we explored in parts I and II of this book relate to what educators teach in reading, how it is taught, and how impactful reading assessment needs to be applied to the specific context of your school. This chapter applies those principles within Tier 1.

This chapter is split into three parts, organized by grade level–team conversations and building leadership–team conversations. First, we provide guidance for reviewing the outcomes of current Tier 1 reading instruction. Next, we explore the opportunities for addressing any Tier 1 needs. Finally, we provide guidance for developing a plan to improve Tier 1 success.

As a reminder, Tier 1 includes those resources that all students receive. It's the high-quality curricular materials, instructional strategies, and common assessments in which all students participate.

Grade-Level Team Conversations

Grade-level teams should meet in the beginning of the school year, immediately after the completion of universal screening and then regularly throughout the school year to review student growth on both progress-monitoring data and middle- and end-of-year screening assessments.

Tier 1 Discussion

Before reviewing Tier 1 data, teams can set the stage for Tier 1 data review by engaging in a discussion like the one in "A.13: Tier 1 Discussion" (page 149). Facilitate the discussion as a setup to why Tier 1 practices will be the focus of reading improvement work.

Reviewing Current Reading Outcomes

The reading outcomes in any school are a result of the current reading practices teachers employ in each classroom and the system that supports that instruction. Therefore, the first step in improving reading outcomes is to reflect on current reading data. To review the current success of Tier 1 reading instruction, universal screening is needed. Universal screening is the application of screening for all students within a grade. Because of its technical adequacy, described in chapter 3 (page 33), it lends itself well to these discussions. When engaging in these discussions, many teams like to start with an all-educator conversation to reflect on the importance of Tier 1 and how Tier 1 practices impact student outcomes. The "A.13: Tier 1 Discussion" for all educators activity (page 149) is designed to support those conversations.

Because system-level changes require consistent practices and system-level resources, expecting individual teachers to review and act on data is not expected to result in lasting, schoolwide change. Therefore, we provide guidance and tools for grade-level teams to review data.

We recommend a grade-level team session focused on reviewing universal screening data for Tier 1 needs immediately after the collection of those data. We strongly suggest keeping this meeting separate from the meetings where you consider Tier 2 and 3 needs, as we have found once teams shift to planning for interventions, it's hard to return to Tier 1. During that time, teachers engage in the Collaborative Improvement Cycle (introduced in chapter 4, page 47) using data protocols and common team agendas to support their work and ensure they are able to move from explaining data to using data. A key consideration is the percentage of students who score below expectation on universal screening. If Tier 1 instruction isn't meeting the needs of the vast majority of students, too many students will need intervention. We suggest identifying the gap as the difference between 100 percent of students expected to reach expectations and the actual percent in each grade level.

"B.1: Grade-Level Team Agenda Tier 1" (page 156) provides a structure for that meeting. After identifying team roles and reviewing the agenda with the team, the team engages in the first step of the Collaborative Improvement Cycle: Gap Identification, divided into three parts. "B.2: Grade-Level Team

Protocol Tier 1 Gap Identification" (page 158) provides a data protocol aligned to this agenda that includes the following steps.

1. Teams review current student screening data to identify overall Tier 1 success (defined as meeting the needs of roughly 80 percent of the students).
2. Teams consider how equitable Tier 1 outcomes are across student groups. Teams can ignore those rows in which they don't have students in those student groups in their community.
3. Teams consider if they have potentially overidentified students as having a specific learning disability by comparing it to the state average. Schools that have a large proportion of students identified as having a specific learning disability should consider if Tier 1 reading instruction is impacting these rates.
4. Teams then summarize current reading data using a summary statement designed to streamline considerations during the next step of the cycle.

Each team meeting agenda also contains a bar showing the ratio of time in the meeting to devote to each step of the Collaborative Improvement Cycle (see figure 6.1). It can be easy to spend all the time in a meeting discussing data; we want to ensure you get to the action planning portion of the meeting. To that end, it's helpful for the team facilitator to plan the specific times for each portion of the meeting using that bar as a reference. Parts of the agenda that will likely require more time to discuss represent larger portions of the bar. For instance, in figure 6.1, gap analysis is expected to take the largest portion of meeting time. Without a plan for how much time to spend on each part of the meeting, teams often find they don't get to the action planning part of their work.

Tier 1 Data Review Meeting Part I
Grade-Level Team Agenda

Team Roles

Role	Today's Talent
Facilitator	
Timekeeper	
Note taker	
Discussion leader	

Gap Identification	Gap Analysis	Action Planning

Agenda

Topic	Task	Time	Notes
Agenda review	• Review agenda • Set team roles		
Tier 1 gap identification	Is Tier 1 implementation effective for students in our grade?		

Figure 6.1: Bar depicting ratio of time during team meetings.

Grade-Level Team Meeting Tools

"B.1: Grade-Level Team Agenda Tier 1" (page 156) provides a structure for the Tier 1 discussion meeting. "B.2: Grade-Level Team Protocol Tier 1 Gap Identification" (page 158) provides a data protocol aligned to the Tier 1 meeting agenda.

Grade-Level Team Protocol Tier I Gap Analysis

The "B.3: Grade-Level Team Protocol Tier 1 Gap Analysis" (page 160) provides a data protocol aligned to the gap analysis step in the Grade-Level Team Tier 1 Agenda.

Analyzing Gaps

Once teams identify gaps they want to address, it can be tempting to jump directly to action planning to address those gaps. Every school setting is different. Educator expertise, roles, curricular resources, schedules, and more all impact the success of Tier 1 reading instruction. For that reason, teams need to take time to consider the specific opportunities for improvement before developing plans. The second half of the Part 1 agenda addresses that analysis.

The gap-analysis step is included in the "B.1: Grade-Level Team Agenda Tier 1" (page 156). During this discussion, teams conduct a gap analysis based on their current data and consensus, then prioritize those gaps they need to plan to address. "B.3: Grade-Level Team Protocol Tier 1 Gap Analysis" (page 160) provides a data protocol aligned to that gap analysis. Potential gaps are organized by the MTSS levers for system change explored throughout this book (see table 6.1). Let's explore each.

Strategic Leadership and Teaming

Teams are integral to successful, lasting reading improvement. Not only do they ensure that the correct perspectives and expertise are included in decisions, but they also support building collective teacher efficacy through strategic data use and conversations. Ensuring that both building leadership teams and grade-level teams have appropriate engagement and representation is, therefore, critical to ensure two-way communication and consistency of practices.

As important as it is to have teams, it is more important to ensure the teams have purposeful time to address data and reading needs. When teachers complain about too much testing or indicate that data collection is just paperwork, it is a telltale sign that leadership has not provided them with enough time to review and use the data they collect.

Collaborative Improvement Cycle

Teachers may only review screening data a few times a year; therefore, it can be inefficient for them to remember questions to ask for data analysis and decisions to make for action planning when they use the data so infrequently. Data protocols are valuable because they provide teams with the questions to ask, and they ensure that conversations are effective and efficient by

Table 6.1: Potential Gaps in Tier 1 Success Organized by MTSS Levers for System Change

System Levers for Change	Questions to Consider
1. Strategic leadership and teaming	Do we have the right team members on the building leadership team and the grade-level teams to ensure needed expertise, perspective, and consensus?
	Do teams have regular time to address reading needs and act on reading data?
2. Collaborative Improvement Cycle	Do building leadership teams and grade-level teams use data protocols that guide their use of the Collaborative Improvement Cycle?
	Do teams have experts in the Collaborative Improvement Cycle supporting their data use?
3. Effective and equitable tiered supports	Are we able to spend at least 90 to 120 minutes in reading instruction daily?
	Do we have a clear scope and sequence for teaching reading skills?
	Do we have protected time in the schedule each day for Tier 1 instruction?
	Are instructional strategies clear and evidence based?
4. Impactful assessment system	Do grade-level teams have access to screening data and protocols to support use of those data?
	Do we use formative assessment to inform our daily instruction?
	Do grade-level teams have data protocols to support use of schoolwide reading data?
5. Targeted professional learning	Have all grade-level teachers been trained in, and feel confident around, evidence-based instruction aligned with the science of reading?
	Have all grade-level teachers been trained in, and feel confident in, using our curricular materials?
	Do all educators have access to coaching resources to drive improved reading outcomes?

focusing discussions on those topics best poised to impact student success. For example, a data protocol that encourages teams to consider the MTSS levers for system success when students aren't making enough progress can keep discussions from wandering toward inalterable variables such as family engagement. Similarly, having experts on the team who can facilitate when questions arise and provide perspective on the most important next steps can make regular data use more effective.

Effective and Equitable Tiered Supports

The instruction all students receive needs to be designed to lead to equitable growth and outcomes. Likewise, combined with that Tier 1 support, interventions need to be effective at closing the learning gap for the students who need to make accelerated growth to be successful readers. The needs of the students in your class this year should drive that instruction and may result in different schools within the same district needing different Tier 1, Tier 2, and Tier 3 supports.

A large part of overall reading success is the structure and supports a school provides as part of Tier 1. Considering (1) the schedule and its resources, (2) curricular materials and instructional strategies, and (3) classroom management can support reading success, improving the effectiveness and equitability of outcomes for all.

> Teams are integral to successful, lasting reading improvement. Not only do they ensure that the correct perspectives and expertise are included in decisions, but they also support building collective teacher efficacy through strategic data use and conversations.

Schedule and Its Resources

The schedule is one of the most challenging barriers to success that administrators face. It is a daunting task to create a schedule that supports the variety of learning priorities and student needs within a school. When planning for reading success, consider a few recommendations. The first is to have a schoolwide schedule. A schedule allows for intentional use of resources in a variety of flexible ways. At the very least, at the elementary level, all students within a grade level should be focused on reading at the same time. To facilitate flexible use of resources, it may not be possible for two grades to teach reading at the same time.

Another recommendation is to schedule at least 120 minutes of reading instructional time each day at the K–2 level and at least 90 minutes of reading instruction at grade levels 3–5 (Meadows Center, 2016). The time does not have to be in one block, but the schedule should specify the reading domains taught during each time period (for example, vocabulary and comprehension, phonics, and phonemic awareness, and so on) (Underwood, 2018). The amount of time needed for Tier 1 is based on student data and may not be the same in each grade or school.

With a schedule that allows a grade level to have common times when they're focused on the same reading skills, buildings can allocate other instructional resources to this time more effectively. For example, a reading interventionist can push in or pull out students from across the grade level with similar needs during the small-group instructional time. Special educators can similarly provide their specially designed instruction that targets individual learning needs for students with word-level reading disabilities during small-group time, as well. Because this schedule is set, the special educator and interventionist know that their schedule will not remove students from the vocabulary and knowledge-building work being accomplished through read alouds scheduled during a different part of the daily reading schedule. This format also allows the small groups to be formed based on student needs, rather than the common practice of taking all students who need intervention from a teacher's room from 10:00–10:30, regardless of the skills those students need to work on.

Curricular Materials and Instructional Strategies

Similar to a common schedule, all teachers should use the same curricular materials and evidence-based strategies for targeted skills for Tier 1 instruction. These should consist of a strong, research-based set of curricular materials that address the five components of reading and include evidence-based instructional strategies that support initial, direct instruction and ongoing, embedded, intentional practice to support students in various stages of learning skills. These materials and routines allow teachers to focus on differentiating for individual student strengths and weaknesses, otherwise known as the art of teaching, while not having to focus on creating materials to ensure they address the science of teaching students to read.

Reflect on the instructional hierarchy discussed in chapter 2 (page 19). Curricular materials should support students when they are first learning accuracy with skills by focusing on explicit instruction. Strategies that incorporate elements of direct, explicit instruction should be embedded into those components of lessons. Then, materials should build in several elements of practice embedded into current and future lessons and units to support students to gain fluency in skills and move toward generalization and adaptation.

In schools with multilingual students and English learners, Tier 1 instructional routines need to ensure they address the skill needs of these students (Cárdenas-Hagan, 2020). For example, within a phonics skill teaching routine that includes modeling a phonics skill, guided practice with several words, including the phonics skill, and then independent practice using the skill with immediate feedback, the teacher would modify the routine to add in a brief discussion of each word being practiced. The teacher would define the word, give examples and nonexamples, and then connect to the students' home language by asking what the word is in that language and discuss how it's similar to or different from the English word. That brief change to the teaching routine supports language development and the language comprehension component of the simple view of reading that multilingual students need.

Teachers can rely on the instructional hierarchy to practice the art of teaching within and across lessons. Students who are still acquiring the new skill can be given more instruction and those who are accurate but slow can be given more practice. Teachers also ensure that the practice activities they provide for students to work on individually or with a partner are appropriately matched to skills students have already gained accuracy with.

A note about fidelity within Tier 1: The instruction educators provide has the biggest impact on student learning. Adult implementation, including aligning that instruction with the concepts explored in chapters 1 and 2 of this book, have the potential to accelerate growth for all learners. To that end, as districts adopt new curricular materials aligned with reading research, school leaders often require these core reading programs to be implemented exactly as written, otherwise described as with fidelity. Identifying those things that will be consistently implemented across classrooms is an essential part of the work. However, this may or may not include all the components of a new set of curricular materials. Before evaluating teacher implementation of core programs, we suggest grade-level teams consider the following.

1. The evidence base of the program (as well as the individual lesson components of the program)
2. The match of the program to the needs of local students
3. The schedule, professional learning, and ongoing coaching provided to educators to implement the program as designed
4. How the program can be differentiated and intensified to meet individual and group needs

By considering these specific factors, school teams (including building leadership and grade-level teams) can identify specifically what instructional components are consistent across classrooms and how teachers will use the assessment data to adequately address student needs by intensifying and differentiating reading instruction using the concepts described in chapters 1 and 2 (pages 11 and 19) of this book. Rigid fidelity to a program and adherence to pacing guides may not result in improved reading outcomes for all if the program and pacing is not aligned to students' current skill levels.

Support Classroom Management

One of the top barriers to effective instruction reported across schools we work with is classroom management. We suggest addressing classroom management during reading instruction in two main ways. First, through clear expectation setting and reinforcement of appropriate behavior. The Good Behavior Game is an evidence-based way to teach expected behavior, reinforce its use, and teach students to monitor their own behaviors (Kellam et al., 2011).

In addition to teaching and reinforcing expectations, engaging, explicit instruction is also a way to support classroom management. As described in chapter 2 (page 19), when lessons are paced in a thoughtful manner, students respond many times each minute of instruction, and it's more challenging for them to be off task. Table 2.4 in chapter 2 (page 28) outlines several examples of active engagement activities during instruction. Likewise, Kevin Feldman defines engaging instruction as what students are saying, writing, or doing (Feldman, 2018). This definition focuses less on the topic of instruction, or the "show," so to say, that teachers are performing. When students are engaged, that is, when they are speaking or writing during a lesson, they are also, then, highly likely to be on task and less likely to be distracted or behaving inappropriately.

Impactful Assessment System

As we've previously discussed, data protocols to support using assessment data are critical. Simply having assessments that address each purpose (screening, diagnostic, and so on) is not enough. Educators need time to interpret and use those data to drive reading instruction. Data collection without leveraging those data for student and system needs is incredibly inefficient.

Targeted Professional Learning

Not only do schools need plans to support incoming teachers to learn their reading curricular materials well, but they also need to plan to support veteran teachers to address questions and needs as they arise.

Modern technology is fantastic! New refrigerators, for instance, come with many more features than they did even five years ago. When you get a new kitchen appliance, there are certain things you learn to do immediately. You make sure the freezer and refrigerator are at the right temperatures and check that the icemaker is making ice. After you get started with the new refrigerator, though, your learning doesn't end. After a few months, a light may come on, indicating a filter needs to be changed. At that point, you may get out the manual or find an online video to continue your learning.

When teachers implement a set of curricular materials, questions arise. Maybe a specific routine doesn't seem to be working to help students learn, or a teacher wonders why a particular part of the lesson needs to be included each day, and they have an idea for something that may be more appropriate for their learners. In these situations, it doesn't help teachers to wait for the next professional development day or their next monthly meeting with an instructional coach. They need regular, ongoing opportunities to address needs and questions. This can take the form of a coach joining each grade-level team once a week or the grade-level team itself having time dedicated to addressing the implementation of reading curricular materials.

A district leader recently reminded Sarah of the phrase Brené Brown uses in the book *Dare to Lead* (2018): "Clear is kind." This applies to so many parts of education, but we believe it is extremely helpful (and kind) to provide educators with explicit connections between their materials and their knowledge of the science of reading and evidence-based instruction. One way to do this is to provide a guide with screenshots of routines or parts of lessons and add connections between those routines and their background knowledge. These can be shared during team time or all-staff meetings. An example using a phonics curriculum from 95 Percent Group (2024) is shown in figure 6.2.

Action Planning

Once you have prioritized specific areas to improve, you will develop a plan to address identified Tier 1 needs immediately within Tier 1 instruction. Grade-level teams will use the data protocol found in the "B.4: Grade-Level Team Action Plan" (page 162). The gap analysis and resulting priorities should drive the action items. Grade-level teams should consider their resources and barriers when determining action items. For example, a fourth-grade team may identify that they lack expertise in using data on their team and find that, at times, their team meetings stall out because of questions and concerns with their data. Given that finding, they may make an action item of inviting the instructional coach to join their team meetings on days they're reviewing universal screening or progress-monitoring data for the specific purpose of serving as their meeting discussion leader. A primary consideration at this

Now it's your turn.
Turn to page 121 in your Student Workbook. Decide if each word is a closed or a silent-e syllable. Then, write it under the /ī/ ice or /ĭ/ itch column.

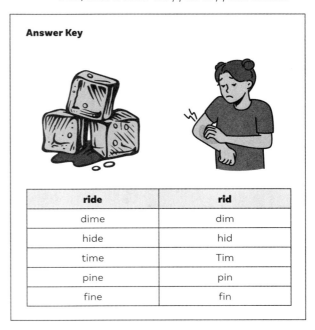

ride	rid
dime	dim
hide	hid
time	Tim
pine	pin
fine	fin

This is an example of you do, or unprompted practice. Students work independently, then share their answers in pairs if in a large group, or through a choral response during small-group instruction. Note that it's not independent practice because the teacher is able to immediately correct any errors.

Source: *Graphic from* 95 Phonics Core Program® Grade 1, Teacher's Edition. *Used with permission from 95 Percent Group*™.

Figure 6.2: Making connections example.

stage of planning is to use the percentage of students who are at risk to determine which essential skills should be taught in whole-group versus differentiated, skill-based groups. If many students are struggling, skill-based groups may be more effective. If most students are on track, whole-group instruction may be sufficient. See figure 6.3.

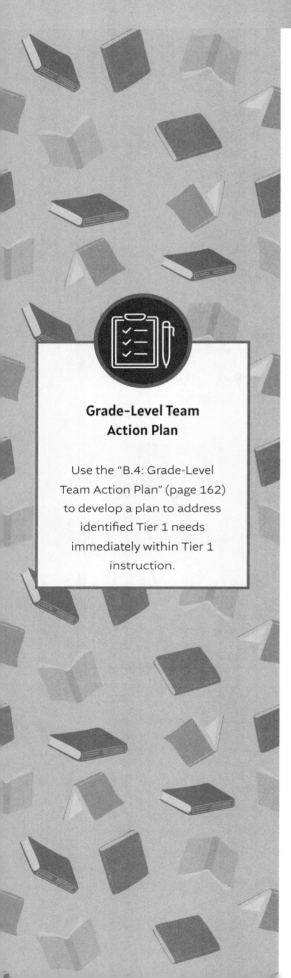

Grade-Level Team Action Plan

Use the "B.4: Grade-Level Team Action Plan" (page 162) to develop a plan to address identified Tier 1 needs immediately within Tier 1 instruction.

Action Item	Who will ensure this gets completed?	When will we implement the action?	How will we monitor that it is implemented?
Teach team a partner strategy for Tier 1 intervention	Instructional coach	Next Monday at team meeting	At the meeting with the agenda
Model Tier 1 intervention strategy for teachers who want it	Instructional coach	Next week	At the meeting with the agenda
Discuss Tier 1 intervention use	Whole team	Two weeks during grade-level team meeting	At the meeting with the agenda

Grade-Level Team Action Plan
Purpose: Decide and document next steps based on gap analysis and identify resources needed to improve our success.

What data will we use to determine if this plan is effective?
Student screening data at middle-of-year screening

When will we evaluate the effects of our plan?
Middle-of-year screening

What additional support does the grade-level team need from the building leadership team to implement the action plan?
None at this time, but may need some release for teachers to observe other grade-level teachers implementing in the future

Figure 6.3: Sample Grade-Level Team Action Plan.

The Lead to Succeed example that follows demonstrates one grade level's discussion around gaps and next steps. Because the gap analysis you conduct is specific in nature, the actions you might take should hopefully be easier to identify than if you went directly from gap identification to action planning. For example, if a grade-level team identifies that the current pace of instruction won't allow them to get through all units in the curricular materials by the end of the year, their action may be to compare the scope and sequence within the materials to grade-level learning targets and identify lessons or units that may be superfluous. If the grade-level team decides Tier 1 is of larger concern, engaging in the Collaborative Improvement Cycle more deeply for Tier 1 may be necessary (Gibbons, Brown, & Niebling, 2019).

LEAD TO SUCCEED
Gap Analysis to Support a Responsive Tier 1

Two years ago, your school adopted a research-based reading curriculum to implement in K–5. Last year, several teachers participated in science of reading training and are becoming more confident in using the materials and how they support implementation of evidence-based reading instruction.

The first-grade team identified that, while their rate of students who meet screening targets has improved over the past year, it's still not strong. And they see student group gaps for their students who are economically disadvantaged.

Several of the first-grade teachers are concerned that the first-grade materials address too many phonics skills and predict they won't teach all units by the end of the school year. They also indicate that their students seem to know the skills during a unit but then forget them a unit or two later.

Using the "B.3: Grade-Level Team Protocol Tier 1 Gap Analysis" data protocol (page 160), the team believes that there isn't enough practice embedded within their reading materials and that two of the units overlap with learning targets they expect in second grade. They recommend removing those units and adding additional practice routines; the instructional coach offers to find appropriate decodable books matched to each skill to support teachers to implement that additional practice.

—

The team in this scenario proactively identified concerns within their curriculum and pacing for the year through formative data and their background knowledge of the science of reading. Their partnership with the instructional coach allowed them to get resources that will lead to a better-designed Tier 1 that will ensure they teach the first-grade learning targets and that students master the skills they teach.

—

Reflect and Connect

1. How might gap analysis support teachers to consider the potential Tier 1 needs in your school?
2. How does teacher background knowledge impact how they implement the science and art of teaching reading in your school?
3. How does "B.1: Grade-Level Team Agenda Tier 1" (page 156) support teachers to move from explaining data to acting on it?

Building Leadership Team Conversations

Building leadership teams conduct parallel system data conversations using their own agendas and protocols. This allows the team to be able to identify needs across grade levels and consider local resource allocation based on current student reading achievement and growth.

Reviewing Current Reading Outcomes

Building leadership teams also engage in reading data review. Using "B.5: Building Leadership Team Agenda (page 163), building leadership teams first engage in gap identification by considering the effectiveness and equitability of Tier 1 reading instruction. They also consider current student growth and specific learning disability identification levels. "B.6: Building Leadership Team Protocol Gap Identification" (page 165) provides a data protocol aligned to that agenda.

Analyzing Gaps

Building leadership teams also conduct gap analysis, but their analysis is slightly different from that of grade-level teams. Since grade-level teams have the most information about implementation and resources within their grade level, the building leadership team reviews the gap analysis and action plan of the grade-level team when conducting their own gap analysis. B.7: Building Leadership Team Protocol Gap Analysis" (page 167) is a data protocol aligned to this gap analysis to support the building leadership team in this part of their reading data review meeting.

Action Planning

Action planning also looks different for building leadership teams than it does for grade-level teams. The role of the building leadership team is to support the grade-level team and remove barriers to their success. Building leadership teams should review the action plan from the grade-level teams to identify ways they can provide support. Some examples of building leadership support to grade-level teams include the following.

» Providing a floating substitute to allow teachers time to observe instructional routines their peers are using

» Providing experts to join team meetings

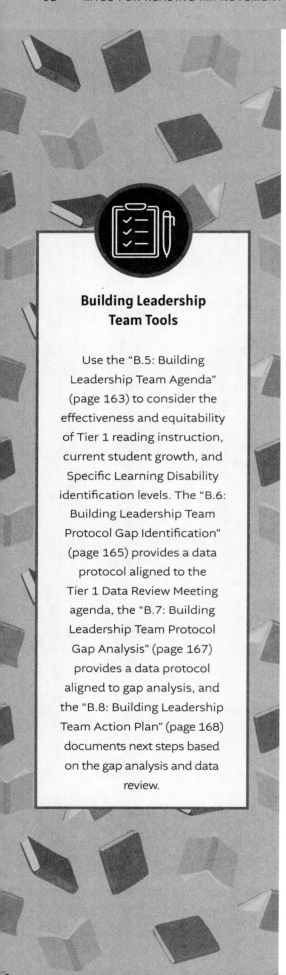

Building Leadership Team Tools

Use the "B.5: Building Leadership Team Agenda" (page 163) to consider the effectiveness and equitability of Tier 1 reading instruction, current student growth, and Specific Learning Disability identification levels. The "B.6: Building Leadership Team Protocol Gap Identification" (page 165) provides a data protocol aligned to the Tier 1 Data Review Meeting agenda, the "B.7: Building Leadership Team Protocol Gap Analysis" (page 167) provides a data protocol aligned to gap analysis, and the "B.8: Building Leadership Team Action Plan" (page 168) documents next steps based on the gap analysis and data review.

» Providing instructional coaching support to help the grade-level team determine what they can stop doing during their reading block

The building leadership team has access to prioritize and reallocate resources based on the data analysis of grade-level teams to support their reading improvement efforts. "B.8: Building Leadership Team Action Plan" (page 168) supports this work. An example of a completed plan with activities for improving Tier 1 reading outcomes is depicted in figure 6.4.

Building Leadership Team Action Plan
Purpose: Decide and document next steps and support for grade-level teams based on their gap analysis and your data review.

Grade Level	Gap Analysis Summary	Action Item	Who will ensure this gets completed?
K	Some students are multilingual English learners. Our Tier 1 instructional routines within the curricular materials don't directly meet their needs.	The interventionist and school psychologist will modify the instructional routines within the curricular materials to add language comprehension support and share with teachers in cardstock form, hole-punched for rings.	Interventionist and school psychologist
1	This grade level has the largest student group gaps between students with free and reduced programs and those without. They are implementing a Tier 1 intervention.	The school psychologist will share a partner routine they developed last year with the instructional coach to save time in development. They will also offer to help with any classroom modeling.	School psychologist
2	The grade-level team identified appropriate next steps.	None at this time	

When will we evaluate the effects of our plan?
At our building leadership team meeting on October 5

What information needs to be communicated to grade-level teams? To the district leadership team?
Each grade-level team lead will communicate the parts of the plan relevant to their grade level at their next grade-level team meeting.

Purpose: Decide and document next steps and support for grade-level teams based on the analysis of Tier 2 and Tier 3 needs.

Grade Level	Gap Analysis Summary	Action Item	Who will ensure this gets completed?
K	The grade-level team identified appropriate next steps.	None at this time	
1	The grade-level team identified appropriate next steps.	None at this time	
2	The team identified more students than last year who need phonics intervention. They are concerned groups will be too large to make necessary student growth.	The interventionist will join the second-grade team in four weeks to review progress data for the phonics interventions and intensify if needed.	Interventionist

When will we evaluate the effects of our plan?
At our building leadership team meeting on October 5

What information needs to be communicated to grade-level teams? To the district team?
Each grade-level team will communicate the parts of the plan relevant to their grade level at their next grade-level team meeting. The principal will provide a summary of current building leadership data and our plans at the next district leadership meeting.

Figure 6.4: Sample building leadership team action plan.

Summary

Implementing high-quality and responsive Tier 1 reading instruction is the best way to make the most growth in overall student achievement. Taking a system-level approach to reading risk prevention requires valid screening data, and, as importantly, time devoted to using those data. Supporting teams to use data through agendas and data protocols designed to support local data review, while guiding evidence-based actions, provides educators with the tools they need to make a plan to address Tier 1 needs. With these things in place, not only will system-level conversations be more likely to occur, but they will lead to improved collective efficacy to address the needs of all students. The "A.1: Reading MTSS Reflection Guide" (page 126) can support this work.

> Supporting teams to use data through agendas and data protocols designed to support local data review, while guiding evidence-based actions, provides educators with the tools they need to make a plan to address Tier 1 needs.

Ask Yourself...

- How intentional have we been about the design of our Tier 2 and Tier 3 intervention system?

- How are teachers and interventionists currently supported to implement and improve their Tier 2 and Tier 3 interventions? What about new teachers?

- How are teams supported to use screening, diagnostic, and progress-monitoring data to address system-level intervention needs?

- What concerns do we expect local stakeholders to have about analyzing and addressing Tier 2 and Tier 3 needs? How might we address those concerns?

CHAPTER 7
Using Data to Drive Tier 2 and Tier 3 Reading Instruction for Some Students

Prevention of communicable diseases like influenza starts with common, low-cost actions such as frequent handwashing and covering your cough. People who are at high risk of catching the flu, such as older adults and people who work in schools, take the more expensive and resource-intensive step of getting a flu shot. But that doesn't mean they stop washing their hands and start letting people cough on them. People who already have the flu might take the even more intensive step of taking antiviral medications. Like vaccines and medications, Tier 2 and 3 intervention systems offer more resource-intensive support for struggling readers who are not meeting reading goals even though they are receiving highly effective Tier 1 instruction.

Regardless of the strength of Tier 1 instruction, there will always be some students who need additional intervention support to become proficient readers. This chapter explores how district-, building-, and grade-level teams are tasked with using data in the Collaborative Improvement Cycle to design and implement Tier 2 and Tier 3 reading intervention systems. The goal is to create an aligned and integrated system of increasingly intensive instructional support that meets the needs of all students.

> The goal is to create an aligned and integrated system of increasingly intensive instructional support that meets the needs of all students.

Reviewing Current Reading Outcomes: Gap Identification

Even schools that aren't explicitly implementing MTSS have some type of reading intervention. The effectiveness of those interventions is directly related to the way those intervention systems are designed and delivered and can be evaluated by the percentage of students who close the gap via those interventions. If the majority of students who are getting intervention are not catching up, it is difficult to identify those intervention systems as effective.

We recommend reviewing screening, diagnostic, and progress-monitoring data in grade-level teams and building leadership teams. The needs of all readers should be considered when designing Tier 2 and Tier 3 intervention systems. That means the needs of students with reading disabilities, students at risk of reading failure, students who need accelerated or advanced reading instruction, multilingual students, and those who are English learners should be considered when designing Tier 2 and Tier 3 interventions. Members of the building leadership team who serve on the team for each grade can make sure that the grade-level teams are consistently working toward school goals. Also, they can ensure consistent implementation across grades while at the same time allocating school resources based on student needs. Although both *grade-level teams* and building leadership teams will use data in the Collaborative Improvement Cycle to design and implement Tier 2 and Tier 3 interventions, we start with describing this process in the grade-level team.

We recommend a grade-level team meeting focused on reviewing universal screening, diagnostic, and progress monitoring data for Tier 2 and 3 needs after each screening period. At this meeting, the team will engage in the Collaborative Improvement Cycle (introduced in chapter 4, page 47) using data protocols and common team agendas to support their work and ensure they are able to move from explaining data to using data.

Recognizing that the Tier 2 and Tier 3 intervention systems need improvement is the first step. Knowing how effective your current interventions are allows you to plan to do business differently to get a different result for your students. In MTSS, each grade-level team uses student data to evaluate and improve the effectiveness of their Tier 2 and Tier 3 intervention systems. This is different from the old intervention assistance team model where teams formed around the needs of individual students. Also, while those student-level teams still form for designing Tier 3 interventions, it is the job of the grade-level team to design the system of intensive support that will meet the needs of students in their grade and reduce the number who need intensive Tier 3.

The "B.9: Grade-Level Team Agenda Tiers 2 and 3" (page 169) provides a structure for that meeting. After identifying team roles and reviewing the agenda, the team engages in the first step of the Collaborative Improvement Cycle: gap identification, divided into three parts.

1. The first part involves reviewing current student data to identify the overall success of the intervention systems.

2. The second part considers how equitable the outcomes of Tiers 2 and 3 are across student groups. Teams can ignore those rows in which they don't have students in those student groups in their community. Teams then consider if they have potentially overidentified students as having a specific learning disability by comparing it to the state average. Schools that have a large proportion of students identified as having a specific learning disability should consider if reading intervention is impacting these rates.

3. The team then summarizes their current reading data using a summary statement designed to streamline considerations during the next step of the cycle.

The "B.9: Grade-Level Team Agenda Tiers 2 and 3" (page 169) provides grade-level teams with a meeting agenda in which the "B.10: Grade-Level Team Protocol Tiers 2 and 3 Gap Identification" (page 171) is used to create a gap identification summary statement that will guide future improvement to the intervention system.

Analyzing Gaps

Once educators identify a problem, they are sometimes quick to jump to a solution. Our experience indicates that schools can get a slight improvement in reading outcomes by changing just about anything related to their intervention system. However, we recommend focusing on evidence-based practices that are likely to close gaps.

Gap Analysis by Grade-Level Teams

The gap-analysis step is included in the "B.9: Grade-Level Team Agenda Tiers 2 and 3" (page 169). During this discussion, teams use their current data and consensus to prioritize the gaps that they need to address. The "B.11: Grade-Level Team Protocol Tier 2 or 3 Gap Analysis" (page 173) provides a data protocol aligned to that gap analysis. Figure 7.1 (page 100) illustrates how to conduct gap analysis.

Potential gaps are organized by the MTSS levers for system success explored throughout this book.

- » Impactful assessment system
- » Effective and equitable tiered supports
- » Targeted professional learning
- » Strategic leadership and teaming
- » Continuous and collaborative improvement cycle

Table 7.2 (page 101) includes questions to consider in each area of need.

Using Assessments to Target Student Needs

Designing effective interventions starts with using assessment data to identify what the students know and need to learn. Targeting instruction to match student needs is essential for accelerating learning and closing the gap. For students in kindergarten and grade 1, determining current skill level is relatively easy and can be largely seen in the universal screening data. For older students, you will likely need to add diagnostic assessment data to identify the lowest skill in the instructional sequence on which each student needs support. Targeting the lowest skill ensures that students have the necessary prerequisite skills and knowledge to benefit from the intervention instruction.

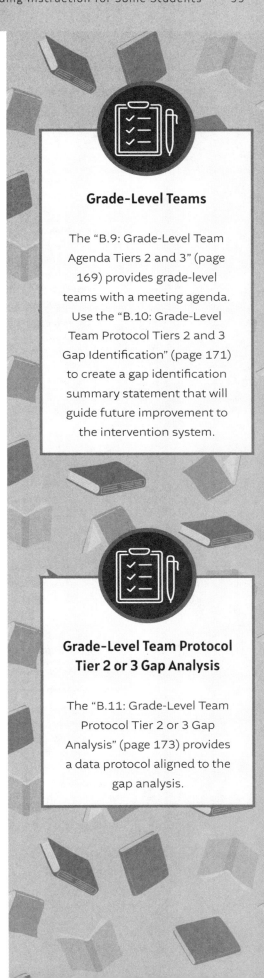

Grade-Level Teams

The "B.9: Grade-Level Team Agenda Tiers 2 and 3" (page 169) provides grade-level teams with a meeting agenda. Use the "B.10: Grade-Level Team Protocol Tiers 2 and 3 Gap Identification" (page 171) to create a gap identification summary statement that will guide future improvement to the intervention system.

Grade-Level Team Protocol Tier 2 or 3 Gap Analysis

The "B.11: Grade-Level Team Protocol Tier 2 or 3 Gap Analysis" (page 173) provides a data protocol aligned to the gap analysis.

GRADE-LEVEL TEAM Tier 2 and 3 Gap Analysis Protocol
Purpose: Identify the extent to which our Tier 2 and Tier 3 intervention systems are effective and equitable.

School	Moats Elementary
Grade	3
Screening Period	Middle of year
Team Members	Third-grade teachers, principal, reading coach, special educator, reading interventionist, English language teacher, school psychologist

Gap Identification Summary Statements:
- Our intervention system is effective for all: _No_
- We expect our intervention system to cause at least 80 percent of the students who receive intervention to be on track toward their goals, but only _50_ percent are making progress
- Some interventions are effective, but these are resulting in insufficient growth: _interventions for students who are not accurate readers_.

For those areas with fewer than 80 percent of students meeting screening targets, consider each of the potential areas of need.
- Impactful assessment system
- Effective and equitable tiered supports
- Targeted professional learning
- Strategic leadership and teaming
- Continuous and collaborative improvement cycle

System Lever for Change	Questions to Consider	Answers and Data	Perceived Need
Targeted professional learning	Have all grade-level teachers, interventionists, coaches, special educators, paraprofessionals, English learning staff, and related service personnel been trained in, and feel confident around, evidence-based instruction aligned with the science of reading? Have all grade-level teachers been trained in, and feel confident in, using our curricular materials?	Interventionists are not trained in effective word recognition instruction.	Yes

Prioritize identified needs. Consider both local data and those actions that are feasible and expected to make the biggest impact on student reading growth.

Top Priority: _Conduct diagnostic assessment_

Second Priority: _Train staff in effective word recognition instruction and how to use the decoding and encoding intervention_

Outline Existing Strengths and Resources. Identify those resources that can be used to address prioritized needs.
- Diagnostic assessment used in K–2
- Word recognition intervention used in K–2
- Training in effective word recognition provided by the state office of education
- Time available for intervention each day

Next Steps. We expect that if we address _matching interventions_ and _our intervention expertise_ we _will increase the students who are successful with our interventions._

Figure 7.1: Sample data protocol.

Table 7.2: Tier 2 and 3 Gap Analysis Questions

System Levers for Change	Questions to Consider
Impactful assessment system	Are screening and diagnostic data used to identify the intervention needs of students in this grade?
	Are screening and progress monitoring data used to evaluate the effectiveness of interventions?
Strategic leadership and teaming	Does the building leadership team provide adequate time in the schedule for planning, implementing, and evaluating reading interventions?
	Does the building leadership team provide adequate personnel for delivering interventions?
Collaborative improvement cycle	Do grade-level teams use data to design Tier 2 and Tier 3 interventions?
	Do school-level teams use data to design Tier 3 interventions?
Effective and equitable tiered supports	Are research-aligned intervention programs available that match the needs of students in this grade?
	Are interventions targeted to the lowest skill in the sequence that the student needs to learn?
	Are students with the greatest skill gaps in the smallest intervention groups?
	Do all students in the intervention group need the same intervention?
	Have the planned number of minutes for Tier 1 instruction been provided each day?
	Are instructional strategies clear and evidence based?
Targeted professional learning	Have all grade-level teachers, interventionists, coaches, special educators, paraprofessionals, English learning staff, and related service personnel been trained in, and feel confident around, evidence-based instruction aligned with the science of reading?
	Have all grade-level teachers been trained in, and feel confident in, using our curricular materials?

Figure 7.2 helps teams visualize the instructional sequence and the relationships between foundational skills and reading comprehension.

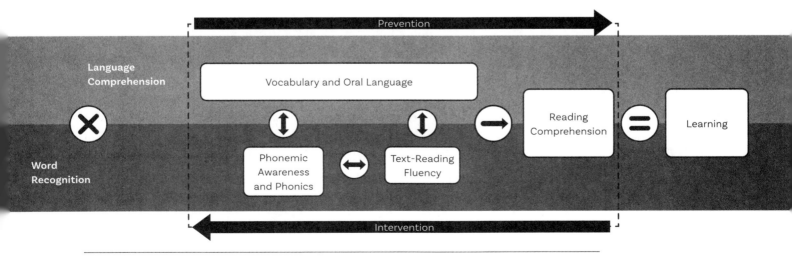

Figure 7.2: The route to reading.

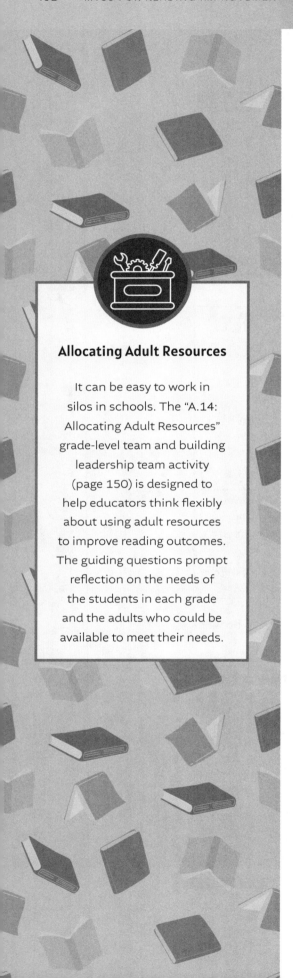

Allocating Adult Resources

It can be easy to work in silos in schools. The "A.14: Allocating Adult Resources" grade-level team and building leadership team activity (page 150) is designed to help educators think flexibly about using adult resources to improve reading outcomes. The guiding questions prompt reflection on the needs of the students in each grade and the adults who could be available to meet their needs.

Grouping

Once the needs of each student are identified, the students can be placed into skill-based groups. Instruction can move at a faster pace when all students in an intervention group have similar skills and needs. When there is more than one classroom per grade, we suggest grouping students as a grade level rather than within each classroom. We recommend teaching the students struggling most (including students with reading disabilities) in the smallest groups taught by the most skilled instructors.

For Allocating Resources

The number of skill-alike groups determines how many adults are needed for intervention in each grade. We recommend flooding the grade with all available adults (special educators, reading interventionists, coaches, SLP, school psychologist, counselor, librarian, paraprofessionals, and so on) so each student who needs intervention is receiving targeted, teacher-led instruction. This approach can be more efficient than asking each teacher to manage several groups within their own classroom and more effective than pulling all students who need intervention from a class at the same time regardless of the skill in which they need intervention. If flexible service delivery is a new concept for your school, we recommend prioritizing a grade or two in which to try it initially. The "A.14: Allocating Adult Resources" activity (page 150) helps grade-level teams and building leadership teams to consider factors related to flexible service delivery.

For Selecting Interventions

The specific needs of the students and the capacity of the school community to implement interventions effectively should determine the intervention programs, routines, and materials that are selected for each grade.

One primary consideration is the skill that students in each grade need intervention on and the number of students who need intervention on each skill. For example, if 40 percent of the first graders can't read CVC words at the beginning of the year, the first-grade team will need to select an intervention program for basic decoding. Or if 60 percent of the third-graders aren't comprehending text because they can't read fluently, the third-grade team will need an intervention to build text reading fluency. In these cases, it may be helpful to use the same intervention program to replace Tier 1 phonics instruction to allow students to receive two lessons with the same program each day.

Another primary consideration for intervention selection is alignment to the research. As much as possible, teams should select intervention programs that have evidence of working to correct the identified skill gaps. In the absence of that evidence, look for programs that contain elements of research-aligned instructional design and delivery.

Once the team identifies research-aligned interventions for each skill gap, they should consider their capacity to implement the program as designed. Considerations include time available for intervention, alignment to the core reading program, time required for planning, cost, availability of training and coaching on the program, and fit with the skill and knowledge level of the staff who will teach the program. These factors don't have to keep you from adopting an intervention program, but acknowledging them at the point of intervention selection helps teams create realistic action plans. The "A.15: Intervention Selection Considerations" activity (page 151) helps grade-level teams select interventions that match student needs and the capacity of adults to implement them.

For Scheduling Intervention Planning, Delivery, and Evaluation

Finding time for intervention is a challenge in every school. The number of students who need Tier 2 and Tier 3 reading intervention in addition to Tier 1 reading instruction will dictate the daily schedule for each grade. A key feature of the tiered model is the additional instructional time provided to at-risk and struggling readers, meaning Tier 2 and 3 intervention is scheduled at another time of day, outside of Tier 1 reading instruction. For example, students who are struggling with word recognition skills will receive two doses of instruction or intervention in those skills each day (Tier 1 and Tiers 2 and 3) while also receiving the language comprehension instruction included in Tier 1. We recommend scheduling classroom instruction and reading intervention first and fitting other subjects around them.

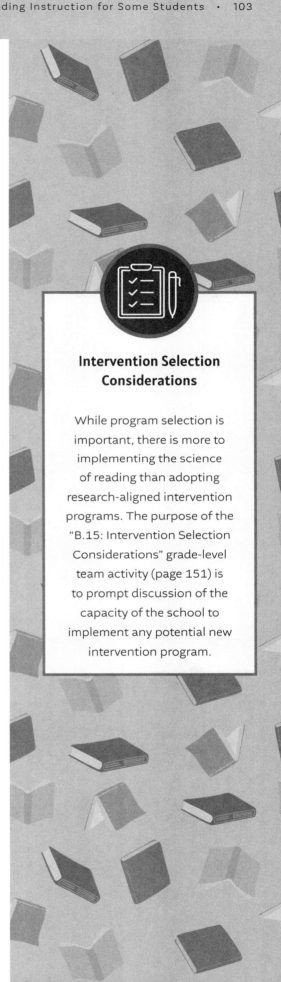

Intervention Selection Considerations

While program selection is important, there is more to implementing the science of reading than adopting research-aligned intervention programs. The purpose of the "B.15: Intervention Selection Considerations" grade-level team activity (page 151) is to prompt discussion of the capacity of the school to implement any potential new intervention program.

Plan to have at least the minimum number of minutes required to deliver the intervention as designed, as well as time for transitions. Remember that staff will need time for professional development to learn the intervention, time to plan implementation together as a team, time to collect progress-monitoring data, and time to review data and consider changes to the intervention. The "A.16: Intervention Scheduling" activity (page 152) helps grade-level teams create a daily, weekly, and monthly schedule for intervention design, delivery, and evaluation. The building leadership team should consider the needs of each grade when creating the master schedule.

For Ongoing Professional Learning

In addition to the previous considerations, the grade-level team needs to plan ongoing professional development and coaching on the implementation of the program. Every adult who is providing an intervention will need training and coaching on the intervention program. The grade-level team can devise a plan for documenting the extent to which the intervention is delivered as designed (a concept called *treatment* or *intervention fidelity*) and supporting the instructor with whatever they need to increase the accuracy of implementation. This becomes important when students who are receiving intervention aren't making progress. Intervention fidelity data will help the grade-level team make informed decisions about next steps.

For Designing Tier 3: Special Considerations

Tier 3 should be the most supportive, intensive, and research-aligned reading intervention available in your school. While it is true that not all students who receive Tier 3 intervention are on IEPs, and also true that students who are on IEPs can be served in all tiers of instruction, the Tier 3 system of intervention should meet the needs of students with reading disabilities.

Additional data sources might be useful when designing the Tier 3 intervention system for your school. These might include data such as the percentage of students on IEPs, disaggregated reading screening and outcome data, and surveys of parents of students getting intervention. Struggling readers, including those with reading disabilities, can learn to read and deserve the intensive support they require to meet reading targets, but systems can't support the intensive needs of those students when there are too many students who need intervention.

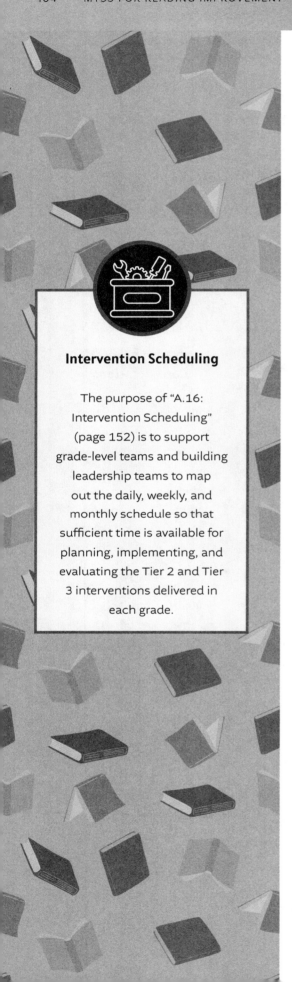

Intervention Scheduling

The purpose of "A.16: Intervention Scheduling" (page 152) is to support grade-level teams and building leadership teams to map out the daily, weekly, and monthly schedule so that sufficient time is available for planning, implementing, and evaluating the Tier 2 and Tier 3 interventions delivered in each grade.

It is more likely that teams will create effective Tier 2 and Tier 3 systems when they take the time to consider the factors outlined here. Each school has its own resources and challenges. The gap-analysis protocol will lead teams to identify their local resources to use to eliminate barriers in the variables described previously. If there are pieces of information about the intervention system that the grade-level team doesn't already have, they may need to collect additional data before moving into action planning.

Once you have prioritized specific areas of the intervention system to improve, you will develop a plan to address identified Tier 2 and Tier 3 needs. Because the gap analysis you conducted was specific in nature, the actions you might take should hopefully be easier to identify. For example, if a school identifies that intervention groups are too large, their action may be to reallocate personnel. The Lead to Succeed example demonstrates one grade level's discussion around gaps and next steps.

LEAD TO SUCCEED
Gap Analysis to Support Effective Tier 2 and Tier 3 Intervention Systems

Two years ago, your school adopted a research-based reading curriculum to implement in grades K–5. Last year, several teachers participated in science of reading training and are becoming more confident in using the materials and how they support implementation of evidence-based reading instruction. This change has resulted in more students reaching reading targets through Tier 1 instruction, so now the team is turning attention to the intervention systems.

The second-grade team identified that, while the students who receive intervention are growing, they are not catching up to grade-level reading expectations. Some of the students who have received Tier 2 interventions are making more progress than students who receive Tier 3 interventions and special education support.

Using the "B.11: Grade-Level Team Tier 2 or 3 Gap Analysis" activity (page 173), the team believes that the Tier 3 interventions aren't aligned to the reading research. The standard protocol interventions used at Tier 2 are not used at Tier 3 or for students who are on IEPs. The staff who provide intervention to the students struggling most (special educators, SLP, and English learning staff) are creating their own intervention lessons rather than using the carefully selected, research-aligned programs used at Tier 2.

The second-grade team recommends intensifying the Tier 2 intervention programs for use in Tier 3. The principal offers to purchase additional intervention materials, and the instructional coach offers to provide professional learning on the programs.

—

The team in this scenario proactively identified concerns regarding the alignment between intervention and reading research across all tiers. The grade-level team conversations will be extended to the building and district leadership teams, which can lead to more effective Tier 2 and Tier 3 intervention systems in this grade and in all grades.

—

Reflect and Connect

1. How might teachers consider the alignment of instruction across tiers in your school?

2. How do silos across departments, funding sources, or roles impact how teachers implement the science of reading in your school?

3. How are the needs of students with reading disabilities considered in all tiers?

Action Planning

Similar to the way student-level teams create an intervention plan or IEP for an individual student, grade-level teams must articulate the specific steps that are necessary to use existing resources to remove the identified barriers to better reading outcomes. Creating the grade-level action plan requires attention to the aspects of asking adults to change their ways of working. It is the role of the school leaders to get the conditions right for all adults in the system to change in ways that result in improved reading outcomes.

Detailed action steps increase the likelihood of success. As noted in the "B.4: Grade-Level Team Action Plan" (page 162), each action item or step should have corresponding information about who will do it, by when, and how the team will know it was completed. The grade-level team should identify the resources the team needs from the building- and district-level leadership teams to accomplish their goal. It is the job of school leaders to provide those resources.

Gap Identification, Gap Analysis, and Action Planning in Building Leadership Teams

In addition to each grade-level team reviewing the percent of students receiving intervention who are closing the gap, the building leadership team should review intervention effectiveness data as well. While they follow the same Collaborative Improvement Cycle steps as the grade-level team, the building leadership team takes a slightly different focus. Building leadership teams focus on resource allocation to grade levels, so they need to compare data across grades to identify the grades in which the intervention system needs further support.

Using "B.5: Building Leadership Team Agenda" (page 163), building leadership teams first engage in gap identification by considering the effectiveness and equitability of Tier 1 reading instruction. They also consider current student growth and specific learning disability identification levels. "B.6: Building Leadership Team Protocol Gap Identification" (page 165) provides a data protocol aligned to that agenda.

Building leadership teams conduct gap analysis, but their analysis is slightly different from that of grade-level teams. Since grade-level teams have the most information about implementation and resources within their grade level, the building leadership team reviews the gap analysis and action plan of the grade-level team when conducting their own gap analysis. "B.7: Building Leadership Team Protocol Gap Analysis" (page 167) is a data protocol aligned to this gap analysis, and "B.8: Building Leadership Team Action Plan" (page 168) supports the building leadership team in this part of their reading data review meeting. By engaging stakeholders in school-level planning, the building leadership team ensures that the needs and concerns of the school community are addressed.

Summary

To achieve the goal of all students meeting grade-level reading targets, the Tier 2 and Tier 3 intervention systems provide the intensive support students need in addition to highly effective Tier 1 instruction. The interventions must accelerate progress in reading and cause students to catch up to grade-level expectations. Grade-level teams are tasked with using screening, diagnostic, and progress-monitoring data to consider the needs of all students, including students with disabilities, students identified as gifted, and English learners when they design and implement intervention systems. Building leadership teams engage community stakeholders to make use of local resources to support grade-level team action plans. The goal is to engineer and sustain an aligned system of increasingly intensive instructional support that meets the needs of all students. The "A.1: Reading MTSS Reflection Guide" (page 126) can facilitate this important work.

Ask Yourself...

- How might you know if your reading improvement efforts are successful?

- Which components of your reading system (Tier 1, Tier 2, Tier 3) are most effective? Which are least effective?

- What are the most common barriers you experience to implementing system-level action plans for reading improvement?

- How will you identify what needs to be improved or intensified when students aren't making the reading growth necessary?

CHAPTER 8
Improving and Intensifying the Three-Tiered Model for Reading Results

Even after designing and implementing strong practices within each tier of support, schools will inevitably have grade levels or groups that continue to struggle to grow reading skills at an equitable and sufficient pace. In these cases, it's imperative to devote time to continue to improve systems to address every student's reading needs. And, yet, in the day-to-day bustle of a school, there is rarely time to reflect on the past when educators are constantly dealing with the present and looking forward to the next priority.

In chapters 6 and 7 (page 81 and page 97) we gave recommendations and tools to help teaching teams and leaders consider the effectiveness of current reading instruction within each tier of support and make a plan to improve outcomes through system-level improvements. In this chapter, we provide guidance for intensifying system-level support for reading improvement efforts when outcomes from action plans are not as strong as expected. We start by completing the final step of the Collaborative Improvement Cycle, outcome analysis, and then we apply principles to consider when intensifying resources across the three-tiered MTSS model.

Analyzing Results of Improvement Efforts

After enacting an action plan, building leadership teams and grade-level teams need to return to the plan periodically to ensure it's having the intended effects. This final step of the Collaborative Improvement Cycle, outcome analysis, allows for reflection, celebration, and planning next steps. For this meeting, grade-level teams will use the "B.12: Grade-Level Team Agenda Outcome Analysis" (page 175), and building-level teams will use the "B.13: Building Leadership Team Agenda Outcome Analysis" (page 177). Both agendas have the same general outline.

> » Teams first review their summary statements to remind themselves of the gaps their plans intended to address.

> Teams review student reading data to consider the student growth that's occurred since the plan has been enacted.

> Teams consider their ability to implement the plan as intended and identify any barriers that have kept them from implementing the plan they initially developed.

> They summarize outcomes of both their student data and the team's implementation information.

> If results have not been what they expected, teams return to the gap-analysis phase of the Collaborative Improvement Cycle, modify their plan, and continue their reading improvement efforts.

Data protocols are available for teams to support this work: "B.14: Grade-Level Team Protocol Outcome Analysis" (page 179) includes both Tier 1 and Tiers 2 and 3, and "B.15: Building Leadership Team Protocol Outcome Analysis" (page 181). Let's dig into specific aspects of this outcome analysis work.

Using Both Student and Educator Data

Student data are the most common information source we have within our schools, and we have a lot of it. In reading alone, we may consider universal screening data, progress-monitoring data, unit formative and summative assessments, grade-level common assessments, state tests, intervention placement tests, attendance data, and behavior office referral data. As you read this list, you may have been adding additional data sources! Because of this, many times, our decisions regarding next steps and intensification are focused on student data alone. However, while student data tell us the outcome of a plan, it doesn't tell us exactly what occurred. Figure 8.1 visualizes this.

Figure 8.1: Inputs and outcomes.

At some point in time, a team decides to use a specific strategy, focus on a specific skill, or implement a specific intervention. Then, after a period of time, they measure student outcomes

---

Grade-Level and Building Leadership Teams

During the Outcome Analysis meeting, grade-level teams will use the "B.12: Grade-Level Team Agenda Outcome Analysis" (page 175) and building leadership teams will use the "B.13: Building Leadership Team Agenda Outcome Analysis" (page 177). To support this work, use the data protocols found in "B.14: Grade-Level Team Protocol Outcome Analysis" (page 179) and "B.15: Building Leadership Team Protocol Outcome Analysis" (page 181).

and conduct outcome analysis. We often assume that we are monitoring the impact of our plan, but, in reality, we're analyzing the impact of the big question mark in the middle.

It may be that we implemented the plan as intended, but schools are complex places, and it can be challenging to do so, even with strong planning and training (Gresham, 1989; van Dijk, Lane, & Gage, 2023). For example, consider a school implementing a new set of reading intervention materials. They offered training for teachers, but it was offered during summer months when teachers were off contract, and several were unable to attend the training due to family obligations. Because of this, the intervention is never implemented as planned throughout the year. Recognizing that we need to consider current practices when evaluating student data will lead to next steps being customized to your local context and needs.

Summarizing Outcomes of System-Level Reading Improvements

With both student and adult information considered, the results of an action plan form a matrix, like the one depicted in figure 8.2.

		Student Growth	
		We had low levels of student growth and / or student group gaps.	**We had high levels of student growth and no student group gaps.**
Action Plan Implementation	**We weren't able to implement many parts of the plan.**	Revisit the plan and request support to remove any barriers to implementation.	Reflect on the actions the team took to achieve this success.
	We were able to implement most, if not all, of the plan.	Revisit gap analysis and improve action plan.	Reflect on the action the team took to achieve this success.

Figure 8.2: Outcome-analysis summary.

There are four possible outcomes schools may experience. Let's consider our next steps given high or low student growth.

High Levels of Student Growth

When experiencing high levels of student growth, we celebrate, regardless of how closely aligned our current actions are to our action plans. In the two scenarios of high student growth depicted in figure 8.2, students made the progress they needed to based on the supports we were able to put into place. We recommend including in those celebrations a reflection focusing educators on their practices that resulted in that growth. What did we implement that impacted student reading outcomes? For example, a team may have focused on getting through five lessons a week for an intervention program that previously was implemented in two or three lessons a week. Or a team may have made a Tier 1 plan to incorporate more practice into each lesson, and, while they weren't able to implement it every day as planned, each educator implemented the additional practice an average of three days each week.

Celebrating student growth in this manner helps teams build collective efficacy. Focusing on the specific actions educators took and their impact on student success, whether for a small-group intervention or the entire grade, builds recognition that our actions have the capacity to improve student outcomes (Adams & Forsyth, 2006). Based on meta-analyses, teacher collective efficacy has an effect size of 1.57 (Eells, 2011), which means students achieve more in settings where teachers believe their actions matter. And focusing celebrations on the specific actions of the team is a great way to build that belief. "B.16: Team Growth Reflection " (page 182) can be used to support teams in these celebration discussions.

Low Levels of Student Growth

When lower levels of student growth are achieved, teams' next steps are directed by what they were able to implement. When implementation is high, the team will return to gap analysis to further improve reading instruction. When it is low, the team needs to consider the barriers that kept them from implementing the plan as intended.

We recognize that there are many barriers that keep educators from being able to implement their plans. It's one of the reasons system-level work is the key to lasting change. When educators encounter barriers, the grade-level and the building leadership teams both need to find ways to remove those barriers to success.

For example, a grade-level team may decide to implement an evidence-based partner practice routine into their daily lessons to boost retention of previously taught skills (a call-back to the instructional hierarchy). One teacher may encounter a barrier that he never has time to add in the routine. Another may find that the time she has to use the routine overlaps with a time that some of her students are pulled out of the class for another service. Both of these reasons for not using the routine are legitimate barriers. In both cases, educators need to be able to share these barriers and generate solutions with their grade-level team. When the grade-level team needs additional support to remove the barrier, they ask for it from the building leadership team.

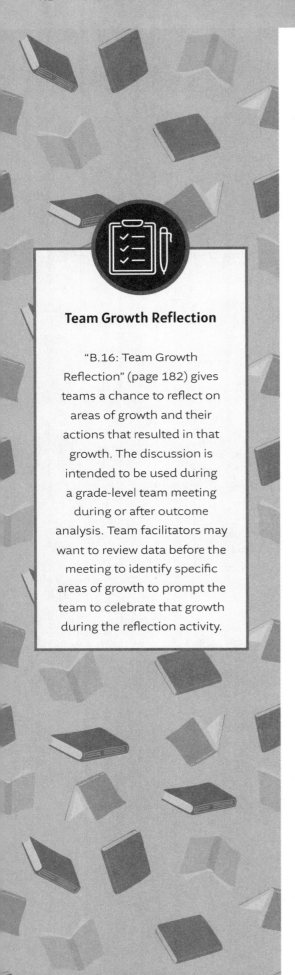

Team Growth Reflection

"B.16: Team Growth Reflection" (page 182) gives teams a chance to reflect on areas of growth and their actions that resulted in that growth. The discussion is intended to be used during a grade-level team meeting during or after outcome analysis. Team facilitators may want to review data before the meeting to identify specific areas of growth to prompt the team to celebrate that growth during the reflection activity.

Other times, teams have implemented their action plans and students still did not grow at the required rate. In those situations, teams must return to their gap-analysis protocol for grade-level teams (Tier 1 or Tier 2, page 160 and 173) or for building leadership teams (page 167). Gap analysis looks similar to the first time teams engaged in this practice, but we'll share some considerations when planning to intensify improvement efforts.

Intensifying System Supports

When considering the intensification of system supports, schools have control over a number of factors that can be intensified to improve reading outcomes, including the materials, instructional strategies, time, group size, alignment, and instructional match (Fuchs, Fuchs, & Malone, 2017). To know which of these to intensify takes conversations and additional information. Table 8.1 outlines each of these factors, as well as some questions to ask and when to consider addressing this factor within your Grade-Level Team Action Plan.

Table 8.1: Factors to Intensify and When to Consider Them

	Questions to Ask	Intensify if . . .
Materials	<ul><li>Do all classroom teachers have research-based Tier 1 materials?</li><li>Do all teachers implementing interventions have research-based supplemental materials?</li><li>Are materials we have being used as designed (for example, all lesson components being used each lesson)?</li><li>Are materials implemented at a pace that will result in completion in the expected timeline?</li></ul>	<ul><li>Research-based Tier 1 materials are not in place.</li><li>Research-based supplemental materials are not in place for interventions.</li><li>Materials are purchased but not used consistently.</li><li>Materials are purchased, but current implementation will not lead to completion of the curricular materials by the end of the school year.</li></ul>
Instructional Strategies	<ul><li>Are reading skills being taught using explicit instruction methods?</li><li>Are intervention methods differentiated based on student need (such as additional practice with immediate feedback)?</li></ul>	<ul><li>Reading instruction in any tier of support is not explicit in nature.</li><li>Interventions are not differentiated and more explicit when needed.</li></ul>
Time	<ul><li>Are at least ninety minutes devoted to reading instruction at the elementary level?</li><li>Is time spent in interventions provided in addition to Tier 1?</li><li>Is there enough time to complete a lesson each session from curricular materials across all tiers of support?</li></ul>	<ul><li>Less than ninety minutes are provided to teach reading.</li><li>Time spent in intervention is not additive in nature.</li><li>It takes more time to complete a lesson than is available during instruction due to the time available.</li></ul>

continued ▶

	Questions to Ask	Intensify if . . .
Group Size	• Are group sizes small enough that the focus of instruction can be targeted to specific skill gaps? • Is there enough time to complete a lesson each session for materials used during interventions?	• Instruction cannot be targeted to specific types of skill gaps (such as fluency or phonics). • A lesson a session is unable to be completed due to the size of the group.
Alignment	• Are interventions aligned with Tier 1 instructional strategies and do skills taught support the Tier 1 learning targets?	• Interventions are potentially confusing students because of the alignment with the focus of Tier 1 instruction (for example, a scope and sequence mismatch).
Instructional Match	• Are interventions aligned with specific student instructional needs (such as phonics or fluency)?	• Interventions are not provided based on student instructional match.

These questions can support your grade-level team as you return to your gap analysis for either Tier 1 or Tiers 2 and 3. The Lead to Succeed example outlines a fifth-grade grade-level team's Tier 1 intensification planning.

Lead to Succeed: Intensifying Tier 1

A fifth-grade team regularly notes that students come to their grade not ready for grade-level literacy work. They struggle to read grade-level content, and many are very slow readers, making it impossible to expect them to read enough content to build knowledge and engage in the critical thinking their standards demand.

Universal screening data at the beginning of this year show that, once again, a large percentage of fifth-grade students are below screening targets. The data also identify a large gap for students who are multilingual and receive English learning services. Through gap analysis, the team realizes they don't have a plan to close skill gaps in an efficient and effective manner. They ask the building literacy coach to join their next meeting and devise a plan to address concerns.

First, they implement a grade-wide, all-school Tier 1 intervention in which educators in every subject spend ten minutes each day with students in an evidence-based partner reading routine. Teachers can choose appropriate content for each day's lesson, and the partner reading provides additional reading practice for all students, distributed throughout the day.

After middle-of-year screening, the team was able to celebrate some student growth, but not as much as was needed to close gaps, and their multilingual learners didn't make equitable growth. They realized they lacked an instructional match to address word reading skill gaps in addition to fluency gaps and to explicitly focus on the needs of their multilingual learners. The team shifted instruction during Tier 1 reading to better meet students' needs. During each reading class they spend twenty-five minutes implementing an evidence-based multisyllabic word reading curriculum that focuses on morphology skills. They've adapted the instructional routines in the curriculum to include vocabulary teaching during the word reading portions of the lesson to address the needs of their multilingual learners. They've had to replace other independent reading and writing work they've done in the past with this but are confident that the explicit instruction in reading longer words that students will encounter when they go to middle school is critical to their success.

—

The team in this scenario recognized that they couldn't ignore reading skills and that building reading proficiency and building vocabulary and knowledge are not mutually exclusive. They built in continual practice throughout the day and implemented a change to Tier 1 that is equitable and effective.

—

Reflect and Connect

1. How do you currently consider student performance when designing Tier 1 instruction?
2. How might universal screening data support Tier 1 planning in your school?
3. How will you ensure that all students can access strong Tier 1 instruction?

Identifying Lessons Learned in Intensification

Throughout our consultation with systems across the United States, we encounter common intensification needs that serve as reminders for things to consider when growth isn't as expected.

Lesson 1: Dosage Matters

When a school has a large number of students who are at risk in reading, they often stretch intervention services to serve larger numbers of students than resources allow. They do well-intentioned things like cut the intervention time in half to serve twice as many students or cut interventions from five days a week to two or three to serve additional students. While this does, in fact, allow the teams to serve more students, it also has the unintended consequence of decreasing the effectiveness of all Tier 2 interventions. Student progress is impacted when their services are decreased. Remember, the best way to improve the effectiveness of the intervention system is by implementing effective Tier 1 instruction. "A.17: Comparing Intensity" (page 153) is an

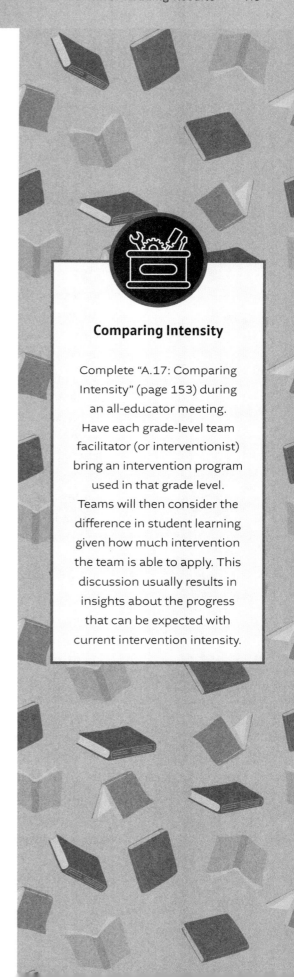

Comparing Intensity

Complete "A.17: Comparing Intensity" (page 153) during an all-educator meeting. Have each grade-level team facilitator (or interventionist) bring an intervention program used in that grade level. Teams will then consider the difference in student learning given how much intervention the team is able to apply. This discussion usually results in insights about the progress that can be expected with current intervention intensity.

activity designed for grade-level teams to review the skills learned if students receive differing levels of intensity of the same intervention.

When interventions don't provide adequate dosage, increasing it can be achieved through increasing the number of sessions a week the intervention is provided or increasing the session length for each intervention. Another way to increase dosage is to make the instruction more explicit and increase student opportunities to respond within the intervention time period (Van Camp, Wehby, Martin, Wright, & Sutherland, 2020). Each of these can increase the intensity of the intervention through increasing dosage.

Lesson 2: Align Instruction With Needs

When schools group students based on schedules, we often see students placed together not because they have similar reading needs but because the schedule best allows for that. This is also common when classroom teachers are expected to deliver all Tier 2 interventions because they will often not have time available to provide multiple supplemental interventions during their day.

The most common situation we see is interventions focused on fluency or comprehension skills when students have needs related to phonics. Remember, most students with reading deficits have needs related to phonological processing (Blachman, 1995; National Reading Panel, 2000). Therefore, especially at the elementary level, but many times at the secondary level, the majority of interventions provided will likely need to address these skills.

Additionally, at times, intervention does not align with Tier 1 scope and sequence or instructional strategies. This can lead to inefficient instruction that doesn't see the same growth as aligned intervention (Stevens et al., 2024).

Lesson 3: Be Intentional About Tier 3 Supports

We know from research that between 95 and 97 percent of students can be proficient readers (Al Otaiba & Fuchs, 2006; Torgensen, 2009). Unfortunately, because most educators haven't experienced that success, many may expect that students who receive intensive services will not close reading gaps regardless of how well those students are served. We're inclined to believe that both the research and teachers are correct. As long as systems require individual educators to provide all intervention (whether Tier 2 or Tier 3), teachers don't have access to high-quality materials, teams aren't given the supports and time they need to learn and collaborate, and systems aren't flexing to meet the needs of students, teacher expectations of growth and outcomes will be true.

However, more growth is possible and should be expected as systems step up to support teachers. And, as systems improve and student data do as well, teacher expectations will shift. Especially with well-planned reflection on the growth achieved and what teachers (and the system) did to drive that growth.

Tier 3 intensity is often impacted by the school schedule, so careful attention to how building leadership teams can support Tier 3 intensification is necessary. Unfortunately, Tier 3 resources are often less intensive than Tier 2, particularly for students with disabilities. Educators we work with regularly report that progress monitoring is collected more frequently, and students receive more intervention time when they receive Tier 2 interventions than when they receive Tier 3 interventions. Often, this occurs when students are receiving specific categories of services, including those for multilingual English learners and those with disabilities. Sometimes when students receive services through these programs, school teams make the mistake of not considering their progress. In some schools it's as if the resources they receive are not considered part of an MTSS.

Additionally, due to scheduling, Tier 1 curriculum and instruction are completely replaced by Tier 3 supports for students in many schools. Students who receive Tier 3 reading supports receive none of the Tier 1 reading instruction provided by their classroom teacher. In this case, what we see is that while student skill gaps may be addressed, they are not making progress in grade-level standards. For example, a student's phonics needs may be addressed, but they are not accessing the rich vocabulary instruction and comprehension being taught through read alouds within Tier 1. These students should receive meaningful access to the Tier 1 language comprehension instruction. Students with significant reading needs need significantly more instruction. By simply replacing one set of resources with another, we diminish student progress. Intentionally addressing Tier 3 system-level needs is critical to the success of those interventions.

Summary

While it can be challenging to find time to review system outcomes and plan for continued improvements, there is little doubt that it is a critical part of an MTSS that drives improved reading outcomes. By considering the implementation and success of Tier 1, Tier 2, and Tier 3 reading instruction, teams can identify the next priorities for improving reading outcomes. The "A.1: Reading MTSS Reflection Guide" (page 126) can facilitate this work. And, by then analyzing needs and choosing improvements based on research and best practices, teams can target specific needs in their systems, just as we do with students.

Because of the power of the MTSS framework to support the implementation of reading-improvement efforts, it is a critical part of enabling educators to improve reading outcomes, the title of this part of the book.

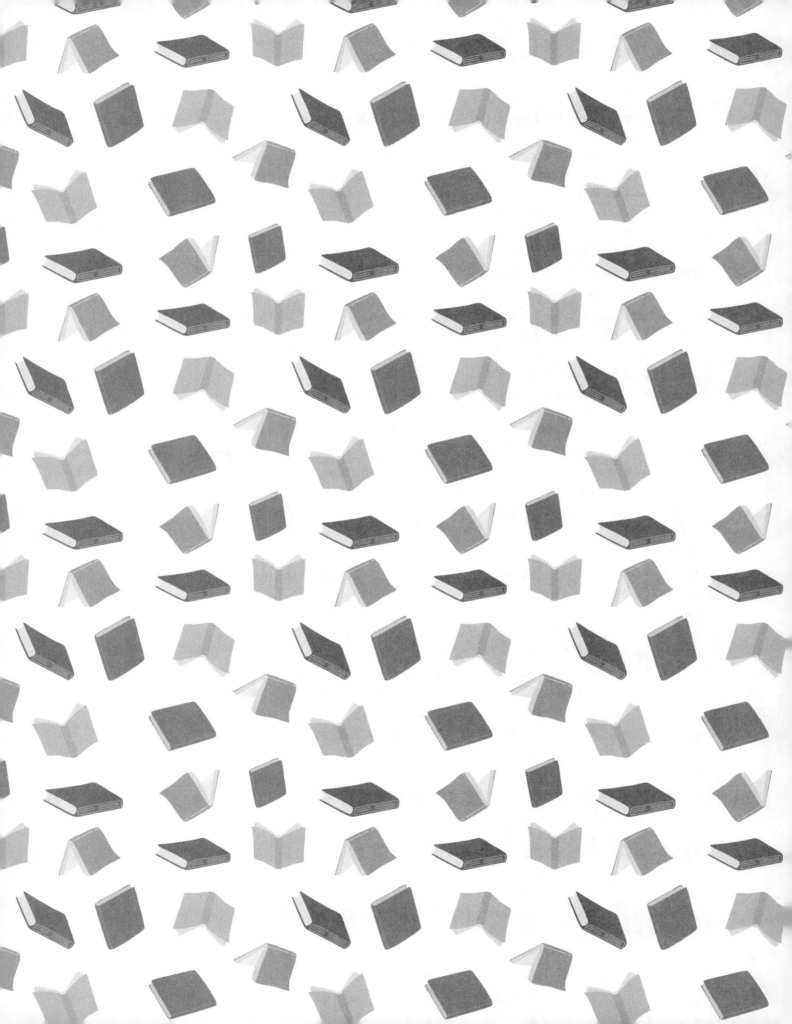

Epilogue

Congratulations! You've explored systemwide reading improvement through an MTSS. We hope that you have gained powerful insights about your school through this process.

Throughout this book, we focused on providing tools and context to aid in system-level improvements of reading outcomes through implementation of an MTSS. It's worth revisiting some of the principles guiding the work we described in the introduction.

Lasting schoolwide change is hard to achieve. As we discussed at the start of the book, schools are complex places with many priorities and factors impacting success. To support lasting reading improvement, selecting the right reading curricular materials or getting training in the science of reading is not enough. Systems need to do the following.

1. Understand reading science
2. Engineer a robust system of support
3. Enable educators to improve reading outcomes

This book is organized into these three parts to demonstrate the importance of the topics each section discusses. MTSS is the vehicle by which schools can support the implementation of reading science and provide the proactive support that is necessary to see results from reading improvement efforts. The following three scenarios explore challenges in current practice that schools today face and provide recommendations using the three parts.

Common Scenario 1

Current Practice

Most teachers have participated in a training on the science of reading, and a year ago, the school updated their assessment system to include high-quality tools. However, educators haven't learned how the expertise they have gained applies to their curriculum, when to use it in the schedule, or what to do when a group of students doesn't respond when they try the practices they learned in their training.

Recommendation

» *Part 1: Understanding Reading Science*—The school has supported educators to learn about reading science. No prioritized action.

» *Part 2: Engineering a Robust System of Support*—Teaming needs to be a priority for this school. Educators need teams with whom they can review their practices and problem solve as needs arise. These teams can also be used to help teachers analyze their curricular materials to understand how they best align with the reading science.

» *Part 3: Enabling Educators to Improve Reading Outcomes*—As part of their teams, educators may also need support in using their data throughout the year to guide their reading instruction and better apply their learning.

Common Scenario 2

Current Practice

A few teacher leaders have participated in training on reading science, and it will soon be offered optionally to all educators in the school. In an effort to minimize time in testing, the school is only giving state-required tests this year, and they don't use the data to guide instruction. The district did adopt a research-based reading curriculum two years ago that all teachers use. The school has not seen meaningful growth from year to year on the state-required tests they use.

Recommendation

» *Part 1: Understanding Reading Science*— The school needs to find a way to give all teachers some expertise in reading science, even if they aren't participating in time-intensive training. One way the school could respond is to allow the educators who do have expertise to align the lesson parts of their curriculum with the reading research and then provide professional learning for all staff in that alignment and provide some of the background knowledge about reading science at that time. Additionally, the school or district should conduct an assessment review to identify any gaps and overlaps within their assessment system.

» *Part 2: Engineering a Robust System of Support*—Teaming needs to be a priority for this school. Educators will need to work in teams to continue to learn about reading science and its application within their classrooms.

» *Part 3: Enabling Educators to Improve Reading Outcomes*—As part of the work of aligning curriculum with the reading science, educators should also learn in their teams how their current, or new, tests align with the reading science and how to use the data to inform Tier 1 instruction and Tier 2 and 3 intervention.

Consider your current reading implementation and outcomes in relation to these challenges and recommendations.

As leaders work to support reading improvements through implementation of an MTSS, revisit the "A.1: Reading MTSS Reflection Guide" (page 126), or another we shared at the beginning of the book. While these self-reviews are often only completed when required by a consultant or a grant, they can support your action planning on an ongoing basis.

While it can be tempting to skip this type of reflection, we find it essential to improvement efforts. It allows teams to build consensus around priorities and opportunities for improvement. Just as important, though, self-reviews provide information about the adult implementation of the science of reading within an MTSS. This gives leadership teams more information with which to make future plans and provides guidance to support gap analysis. If you find that many areas of your system have been identified for improvement, we suggest starting with getting teams in place and using universal screening data in the continuous improvement process.

A Final Activity

As teams engage in the ongoing work of reading improvement, a reflection on learning can be a welcome way to celebrate accomplishments and review important learnings. The "A.18: MTSS World Café" activity (page 154) provides a structure for this conversation.

Summary

We admire your work and commend your decision to tackle reading improvement through an MTSS. We wrote this book with the hope that the ideas and tools provided here support your teams to dramatically improve students' reading skills through considering system improvements aligned with implementation science. By attending to the system and maintaining focus on proactively supporting educators, all students will benefit from your efforts.

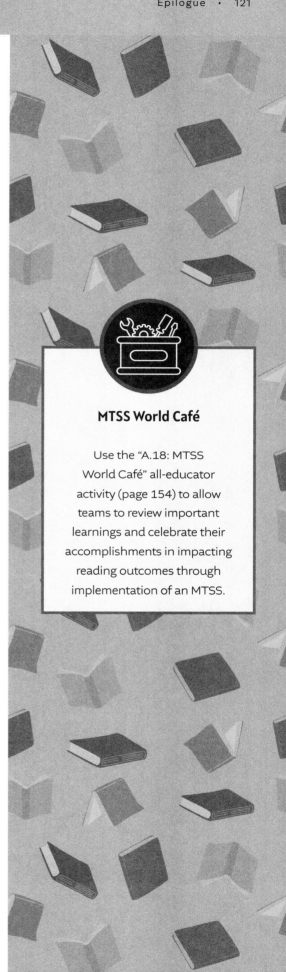

MTSS World Café

Use the "A.18: MTSS World Café" all-educator activity (page 154) to allow teams to review important learnings and celebrate their accomplishments in impacting reading outcomes through implementation of an MTSS.

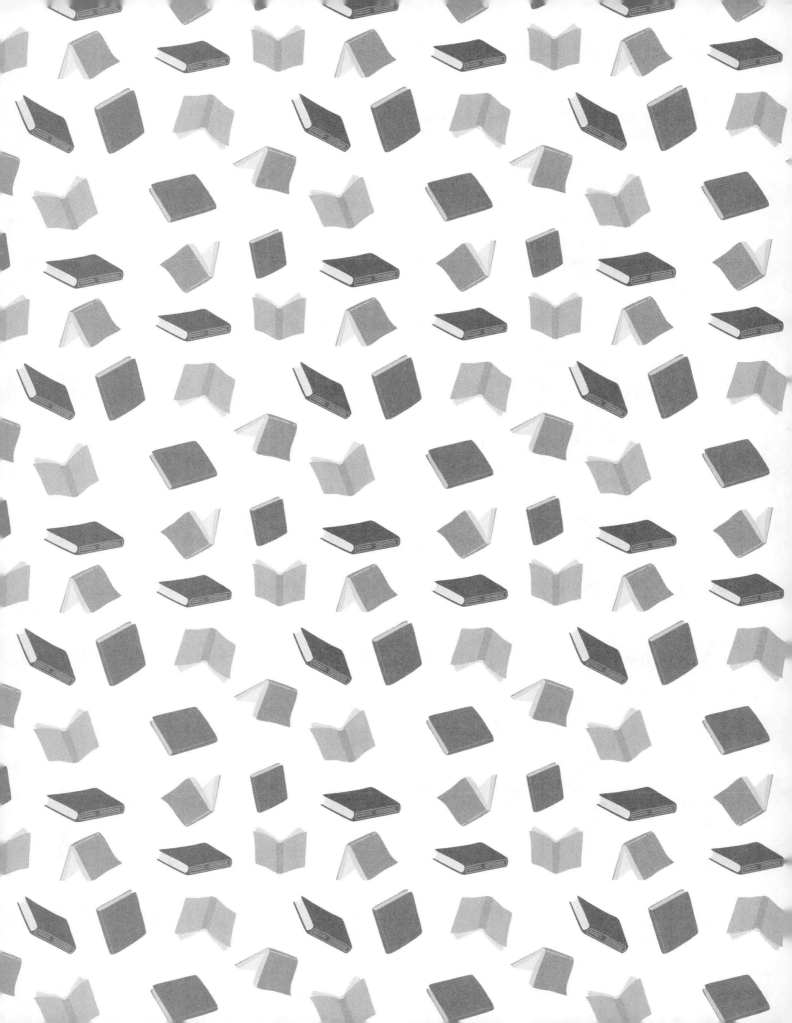

Appendices

Throughout the book we refer to activities and tools to support teams to drive reading improvement through MTSS. The two appendices—appendix A and appendix B—are designed for teams to use to support the three parts of this book: Part 1, Understanding Reading Science; Part 2: Engineering a Robust System of Support; and Part 3: Enabling Educators to Improve Reading Outcomes—those things we know are required for lasting system change.

In the first set of tools, appendix A, you'll find the team activities, reflection tools, and inventories that support system design and educator learning. The second set of tools, appendix B, contains the team agendas and data protocols designed to be used by teams throughout the school year. We separated the appendix into these two sections because, if you're like us, you may want to use individual activities and reflection tools as the need arises and also print the entire year of team agendas and data protocols to share with others on your leadership team.

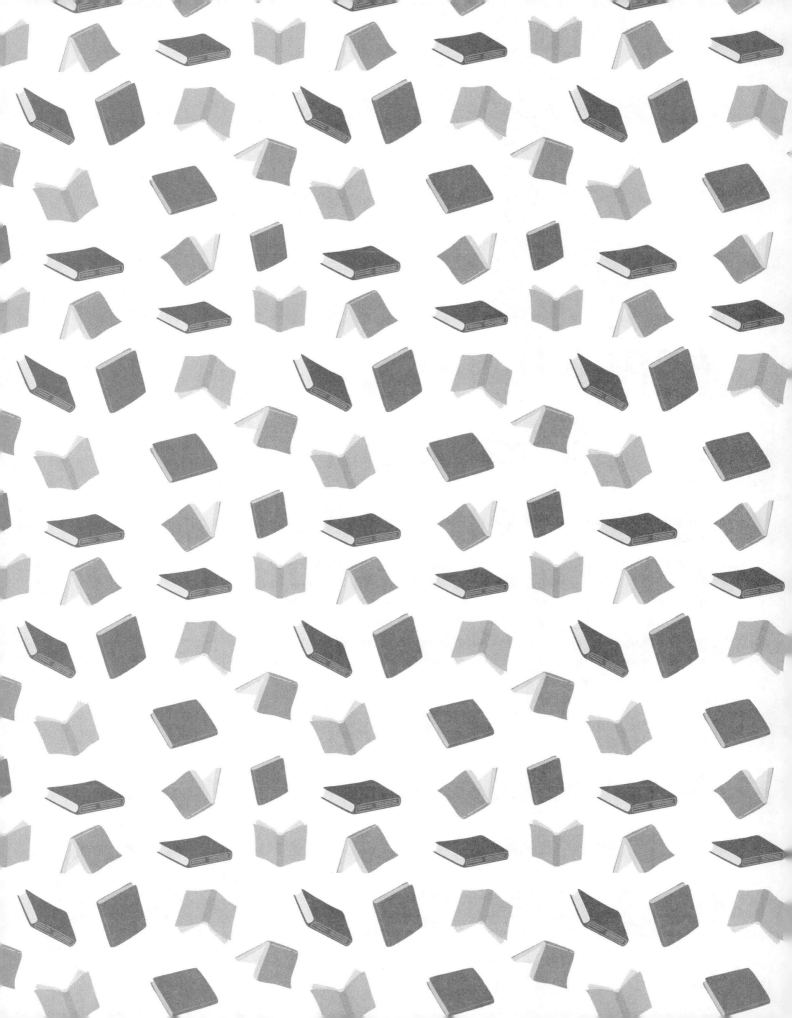

APPENDIX A

Leader MTSS Tool Kit

A.1: Reading MTSS Reflection Guide

Building Leadership Team Activity

Overview
The purpose of this review is to reflect on current implementation of evidence-based practice and set priorities for system improvement.

Activity

1. Provide team members with the Reading MTSS Reflection Guide document (appendix A, page 126).
2. Consider starting with the shaded items. If they are not in place, start with these as urgent priorities.
3. Individually, each team member should reflect on each item and indicate levels of current implementation and priority level.

    Tip: Have each team member bring their copy of this book to refer to items as needed.

4. As a team, review ratings for each item together by team members showing their ratings by holding up fingers (such as one finger for "not yet implementing" and three fingers for "full implementation").
5. The facilitator will count ratings and record the most frequently occurring rating for each response.
6. If there's time after rating, address those items with the largest variance in responses by asking for team members to share their evidence for a specific rating. Re-rate those items to see if changes have occurred.
7. Based on ratings, identify one to three priority items for focus of improvement efforts.
8. Decide communication needs related to grade-level teams and the district leadership team.

A.1: Reading MTSS Reflection Guide

Item	Lever	Effective Implementation	Current Implementation			Priority Level			Chapter(s) Addressing
			Not Yet	Partial	Full	Back Burner	Simmering	Urgent	
Strategic Leadership & Teaming									
1	Team Structures or Membership	The following teams meet regularly to review and act on reading success: • Student-level Team • Grade-level Teams • Building Leadership Team • District Leadership Team Teams are comprised of the following perspectives: • Administrators • Reading experts • Instructional experts • Representation from impacted educators Educators agree current teams are effective and efficient.							5
2	Communication	Two-way communication occurs regularly and predictably within and across the following teams: • Student-level Team • Grade-level Teams • Building Leadership Team • District Leadership Team • Caregivers and the community Educators believe communication is strong.							5
Collaborative Improvement Cycle									
3	Collaborative Improvement Cycle	Teams use the Collaborative Improvement Cycle to review and act on data.							4
4	Data Use Within the Collaborative Improvement Cycle	Teams have time scheduled to use screening data as part of the Collaborative Improvement Cycle. Teams have time scheduled to use progress monitoring data as part of the Collaborative Improvement Cycle.							5 6 7

Item	Lever	Effective Implementation	Current Implementation			Priority Level			Chapter(s) Addressing
			Not Yet	Partial	Full	Back Burner	Simmering	Urgent	
		Collaborative Improvement Cycle							
5	Use of SCIL	Data protocols and team conversations address data on multiple factors impacting student success: • Setting • Curriculum • Instruction • Learner							5 6 7
		Effective & Equitable Tiered Supports							
6	Tier 1	Educators believe Tier 1 should result in equitable growth and outcomes. Tier 1 instruction includes at least 90–120 minutes of reading instruction. All students are included in appropriate portions of reading instruction. Tier 1 instruction is planned by the grade-level team using the Collaborative Improvement Cycle. The Tier 1 core reading program has been evaluated against the reading research. Differentiated instruction is provided during Tier 1 instruction, with whole group and small group formats, as needed. Adherence to planned Tier 1 instruction is monitored by teachers and/or administrators.							4 6
7	Tier 2	Educators believe the purpose of Tier 2 intervention is to equitably accelerate learning and close achievement gaps. The schedule includes 30–45 minutes of daily Tier 2 reading intervention. Tier 2 intervention is matched with student skill and instructional needs by the grade-level team using the Collaborative Improvement Cycle process. Tier 2 intervention programs have been evaluated against the reading research and are implemented per program guidelines (for example, thirty minutes per lesson). Student progress is monitored frequently and regularly. Adherence to planned Tier 2 instruction is monitored by teachers and/or administrators.							4 7

REPRODUCIBLE 129

Item	Lever	Effective Implementation	Current Implementation			Priority Level			Chapter(s) Addressing
			Not Yet	Partial	Full	Back Burner	Simmering	Urgent	
		Effective & Equitable Tiered Supports							
8	Tier 3	Educators agree that the purpose of Tier 3 intervention is to equitably accelerate learning and close achievement gaps. The schedule includes 45–60 minutes of Tier 3 reading instruction each day and can be intensified to match student dosage needs. Tier 3 intervention is planned by grade-level teams using universal screening, diagnostic, and progress monitoring data using the Collaborative Improvement Cycle process. Tier 3 programs have been evaluated against the reading research. Student progress is monitored frequently and regularly. Adherence to the planned Tier 3 intervention is monitored by teachers and/or administrators.							4 7
		Impactful Assessment System							
9	Assessments match purposes	Appropriate assessments are used for the following purposes: • Screening • Diagnostic • Progress Monitoring • Outcome							3
10	Data collection	Data are collected as per standardized instructions in an efficient manner. Progress monitoring data are collected frequently and regularly. Diagnostic data are collected efficiently when needed.							3
11	Use of data	Screening data are used to plan Tier 1 instruction and intervention groupings. Diagnostic data are used to match intervention needs to instruction. Progress monitoring data are used to evaluate the effectiveness of interventions.							3 4 5

MTSS for Reading Improvement © 2025 Solution Tree Press • SolutionTree.com
Visit **go.SolutionTree.com/literacy** to download this free reproducible.

REPRODUCIBLE

Item	Lever	Effective Implementation	Current Implementation			Priority Level			Chapter(s) Addressing
			Not Yet	Partial	Full	Back Burner	Simmering	Urgent	
		Targeted Professional Learning							
12	Training and coaching on how to use the Collaborative Improvement Cycle	Ongoing professional learning, including job-embedded coaching, occurs to support implementation of the Collaborative Improvement Cycle.							3 4 5 6 7
13	Training and coaching on the assessment system	Ongoing professional learning, including job-embedded coaching, occurs to support collection and use of the local assessment system.							3 4 5 6 7
14	Training and coaching on the science of reading	Ongoing professional learning, including job-embedded coaching, occurs to: • Build knowledge of the science of reading. • Support implementation of science of reading instructional design and delivery principles within daily instruction across tiers of support.							1 2

MTSS for Reading Improvement © 2025 Solution Tree Press • SolutionTree.com
Visit **go.SolutionTree.com/literacy** to download this free reproducible.

A.2: Elements of Explicit Instruction

Multiple Uses

Overview

Use the checklist in this appendix to consider the alignment of current instructional practices to explicit instruction, to support the review of instructional materials, or as part of a classroom observation if educators are focused on improving explicit instruction practices as a professional learning priority.

Activity

1. If using the checklist during an all-educator meeting, have each team member identify the elements of explicit instruction that are in place or not in place in their classroom.
2. If using the checklist to review instructional materials, note the elements of explicit instruction that are in place or are not in place in each program.
3. If using the checklist to observe instruction, note the elements of explicit instruction that are in place during the lesson.
4. Use information to identify next steps for improving instruction.

	Element	Description	Examples of What to Look For	In Place?
1	Focus instruction on critical content.	Prioritize phonemic awareness, phonics, text reading fluency, vocabulary, reading comprehension and writing.	Majority of the time is spent teaching the essential early literacy skills.	
2	Sequence skills logically.	Teach easier skills before more difficult skills, teach high-utility skills before less frequently used skills, support students to master prerequisites before teaching the skill itself, and separate skills that might be easily confused.	Letter-sound correspondences are taught in a sequence that allows students to read and write words.	
3	Break down complex skills and strategies into smaller instructional units.	Reduce cognitive overload by breaking down complex skills into smaller units of new material.	When teaching a new phonics skill, instruction includes: • Connecting letters and sounds • Blending sounds into words • Reading words in lists to build fluency • Segmenting and spelling words • Reading the words in decodable text	
4	Design lessons that are organized and focused.	Lessons are on topic, well sequenced, and exclude extraneous information.	Additional stories or examples are avoided if they are not relevant to the skills being taught.	
5	Begin lessons with a clear statement of the goals and expectations.	Communicate what is to be learned and why it is important.	"Today we will learn the spelling for the sound /m/."	
6	Review prior skills and knowledge before beginning instruction.	Use the review of previously taught information to verify that students have the prerequisite skills and knowledge to learn the new skill being taught in the lesson.	Words containing the new pattern are practiced before asking students to read them in decodable text.	

Source: Adapted from the work of Archer and Hughes (2011).

	Element	Description	Examples of What to Look For	In Place?
7	Provide step-by-step demonstrations.	Model accurate production or use of the skill.	"Put your finger under the first letter and say the sound. Put your finger under the next letter and say the sound. Blend the sounds together to read the word. Say the word."	
8	Use clear and concise language.	Use consistent, unambiguous wording.	"Let's practice saying the words that we will be reading. Look at the words in line 1. Read each one with me: *Sam, mat, at, on, man.*"	
9	Provide a range of examples and nonexamples.	Examples and nonexamples communicate when and when not to apply a skill, strategy, concept, or rule.	Examples and nonexamples are provided when teaching students the meaning of new vocabulary words. Ask students to put their thumb up if your statement is an example of the meaning of the word.	
10	Provide guided and supported practice.	Guide students to produce correct responses during the lesson. Once students respond correctly, the teacher can increase the skill difficulty and decrease the amount of guidance and support.	Independent practice includes only the skills the students have produced accurately in front of the teacher.	
11	Require frequent responses.	Have students respond frequently with verbal and written responses.	Choral responding is used to provide a quick review of information when there is one correct response to a prompt or question.	
12	Monitor student performance closely.	Verify student learning by carefully watching and listening to students' responses.	Partner responses, silent signals such as thumbs up, individual turns, and mini white boards are used to monitor the accuracy of responses.	
13	Provide immediate affirmative and corrective feedback.	Respond to students as quickly as possible. Immediate feedback increases the likelihood of success and reduces the likelihood of practicing errors.	"This sound is /i/." "What sound?" Student says, "/e/." "You said /e/. This sound is /i/. Say it with me /i/." "What sound?" Student says, "/i/."	
14	Deliver the lesson at a brisk pace.	Present information at a pace that is slow enough to support students to respond correctly but fast enough that they stay engaged.	Students are actively and correctly responding. Students are not off task in between responses.	
15	Help students organize knowledge.	Use teaching techniques that make the connections between ideas more apparent by organizing and connecting information.	Watch for connections across lessons.	
16	Provide distributed and cumulative practice.	Distributed practice refers to multiple opportunities to practice a skill over time. Cumulative practice includes both previously taught and newly acquired skills. Practice across time helps move new knowledge and skills from working memory to long-term memory.	Students are prompted to use the meanings of new words across the week in their conversation and in their writing. A couple of words with previously taught patterns are included in the weekly spelling test.	

A.3: Reading Tests Used

Grade-Level Team Activity

Overview

To best meet all students' reading needs, tests serve the purpose of guiding instruction. This activity is designed to support your team to understand the tests you rely on to drive effective reading instruction.

Activity

1. Identify all reading tests administered within the grade level, their purpose, and their use.
2. Are there tests some teachers use but others do not? If so, why?
3. How do you feel about the number of reading tests you administer throughout the year? Does it seem like too many or too few? Why?
4. Do you have data that meet all your needs (such as screening, diagnostic, progress monitoring, and outcome)?
5. Are there questions you'd like to know about your students' reading skills that you don't have the ability to answer with your current data?
6. Does it seem like any of your tests give you the same information? For example, do you have two tests that act as reading screening tests?
7. What needs to be shared with your building leadership team regarding your testing system?

Reading Tests Used

Test	Purpose	Administered	Some or All	Analysis and Use

A.4: Building Reading Test Review

Leadership Team Activity

Overview

To best meet all students' reading needs, tests serve the purpose of guiding instruction. This activity is designed to support your leadership team to review the tests used at each grade level and identify gaps and overlaps with expectations and needs.

Activity

1. Choose a grade level.
2. Review the list of reading tests administered within the grade level.
    a. Are there any that aren't on the list you thought were used?
    b. Are there any tests on the list that you didn't expect to see?
3. Review how the tests are used.
    a. Are any used for decisions that misalign with their purpose?
    b. Are there opportunities to use any of the test data for additional uses?
4. For each test, identify if there are gaps or overlaps in assessment purpose.
    a. Universal Screening   Covered   Gap   Overlap
    b. Skill Diagnostic   Covered   Gap   Overlap
    c. Progress Monitoring   Covered   Gap   Overlap
    d. Outcome   Covered   Gap   Overlap
5. How might you explore skill areas that have gaps?
6. How will you address overlapping assessments?
7. Are there any tests that should no longer be used? If so, how will you support educators to use other data to answer their questions currently addressed by those tests?
8. Repeat with each grade level, keeping notes about your needs and next steps.
9. Use the template to make a Building Reading Test Plan of the tests to use going forward.

Building Reading Test Plan

Test	Grade	Purpose	Administered	Some	Building Use

A.5: District Reading Test Plan

Leadership Team Activity

Overview

To best meet all students' reading needs, tests serve the purpose of guiding instruction. This activity is designed to support your leadership team to review the tests used at each building and identify gaps and overlaps with expectations and needs.

Activity

1. Review the list of reading tests administered at each building.
    a. Are there any that aren't on the list you thought were used?
    b. Are there any tests on the list that you didn't expect to see?
2. Which tests need to be consistent across buildings?
3. Which tests can vary between buildings?
4. How might you explore skill areas that have gaps?
5. How will you address overlapping assessments?
6. Are there any tests that should no longer be used? If so, how will you support building leaders and educators to use other data to answer the questions currently addressed by those tests?
7. Use the template to make a District Reading Test Plan of the tests to use going forward.

District Reading Test Plan

Test	Grade	Purpose	Administered	Some	Building Use

A.6: Reasons We Assess

All-Educator Activity

Overview

Assessment has the power to drive the focus of instruction to make it more efficient and effective for all learners. This activity is designed to support a building team during an all-staff meeting to reflect on data use and set the stage for future reading data use in grade-level teams.

Activity

1. Provide teachers with Building Reading Test Plan developed during the Building Reading Test Review leadership team activity (page 135).
2. At tables, have teams discuss current uses and barriers to using each purpose as intended.

   Tip: Consider using a shared document to collect barriers and current uses for review by the Building Leadership Team.
3. Have each table report to the whole group about insights.
4. Share next steps of how reading data use will occur during upcoming grade-level team meetings and ways their data use will be supported.
5. Use a ticket out the door or a poll to collect ideas from educators about supports that would help them better use reading data to guide their instructional decisions.

A.7: Our Programs

All-Educator Activity

Overview

It can be helpful to see best practices in implementation of tiered supports in comparison to current practices. Clearly defining and describing the tiered model and how those systems of support are implemented in your school is an important first step. The purposes of this activity are to clarify the tiered model and start a discussion about the differences between the model and current practices.

Activity

1. Review the description of each tier.
2. Review the description of programs used in each tier.
3. Discuss the similarities and differences between the MTSS model and your current practices.

Our Programs

Program Type	Description of Programs	Our Current Programs
Core	Core reading programs are cohesive and comprehensive programs that serve as the primary tool used to implement grade-level curriculum to all students during Tier 1 instruction. Core reading programs should be aligned to reading research and should emphasize the five essential early literacy skills and writing. The instruction should be explicit, systematic, and sequential, with a detailed scope and sequence. The core reading program should include guidance for the teacher and materials for the students for whole-group and small-group instruction.	
Supplemental	Supplemental reading programs are used to supplement core reading instruction in Tier 1. These programs fill gaps or weaknesses that have been identified in core reading programs, or they provide additional instruction or practice for specific groups of students.	
Intervention	Intervention programs are used with students who are at risk or struggling readers. They are designed to provide instruction that accelerates learning and catches students up to grade-level expectations. Intervention programs are delivered in addition to core reading instruction in Tier 1. Intervention programs are more explicit, systematic, sequential, and provide more opportunities to respond and practice.	

A.8: Reading Instruction and Intervention Program Audit

Grade-Level Team and Building Leadership Team Activity

Overview

It is common for instructional materials to be added across time. When this occurs, it's essential to review their alignment to research, connection to other materials used within and across grades, and their match to students' skills and needs. This activity supports conversations that promote consistency and allow for planned de-implementation.

Activity

1. List the names of programs used in each grade, whether or not they have officially been adopted by the district.
2. Identify the date of the next review and adoption cycle, if applicable.
3. Identify needs and next steps related to consistent use of prioritized programs.
4. Identify needs and next steps related to de-implementation of programs that no longer fit local needs.

Program	Program Type	Grade Level(s)	All or Some Classes	Next Steps

MTSS for Reading Improvement © 2025 Solution Tree Press • SolutionTree.com

Visit **go.SolutionTree.com/literacy** to download this free reproducible.

A.9: Our Teams

Leadership Team Activity

Overview

Teams serve a variety of purposes, and, as team members change, the purpose of teams, their roles, and their communication plans can drift or become conflated with other teams.

Activity

1. For each team, complete the table and answer the questions that follow.
2. Share during an all-educator meeting and keep for future reference when team membership changes.

Team	Purpose	Topics	Members	Meeting Frequency
District				
Building				
Grade Level				
Student				

How do teams communicate within the team?

How do teams communicate with other teams?

How do teams communicate with caretakers?

MTSS for Reading Improvement © 2025 Solution Tree Press • SolutionTree.com

Visit **go.SolutionTree.com/literacy** to download this free reproducible.

A.10: Team Review

All-Educator Activity

Overview

Educators serve on multiple teams and aren't necessarily aware of the teams in the building, who serves on them, and what their purpose is. This makes it difficult to have strong two-way communication. Reviewing teams, and how educators perceive them, can support your decisions about teams.

Activity

1. Give each educator a copy of the table with all building teams listed. Consider using electronic versions so you can aggregate the information later.
2. Have each educator reflect on current team effectiveness.
3. Debrief as a large group, clarifying any team purpose, as needed.
4. Use the information as a building leadership team to inform adjustments to team purpose, process, or membership.

Team Review

Team	How confident are you that you know the purpose of the team?	Is the team worth your time?	Does the team meet at the right frequency?	Should you be on this team?	Should this team exist?
	Very Confident Somewhat Confident Not Confident	Definitely Sometimes Usually Not Never	Meets too much Meets often enough Doesn't meet often enough	I'm a good match for this team. I sometimes need to participate and sometimes don't contribute. I don't need to be on this team.	Yes No Yes, but it may need to change somehow I don't know
	Very Confident Somewhat Confident Not Confident	Definitely Sometimes Usually Not Never	Meets too much Meets often enough Doesn't meet often enough	I'm a good match for this team. I sometimes need to participate and sometimes don't contribute. I don't need to be on this team.	Yes No Yes, but it may need to change somehow I don't know
	Very Confident Somewhat Confident Not Confident	Definitely Sometimes Usually Not Never	Meets too much Meets often enough Doesn't meet often enough	I'm a good match for this team. I sometimes need to participate and sometimes don't contribute. I don't need to be on this team.	Yes No Yes, but it may need to change somehow I don't know
	Very Confident Somewhat Confident Not Confident	Definitely Sometimes Usually Not Never	Meets too much Meets often enough Doesn't meet often enough	I'm a good match for this team. I sometimes need to participate and sometimes don't contribute. I don't need to be on this team.	Yes No Yes, but it may need to change somehow I don't know

MTSS for Reading Improvement © 2025 Solution Tree Press • SolutionTree.com
Visit **go.SolutionTree.com/literacy** to download this free reproducible.

Team	How confident are you that you know the purpose of the team?	Is the team worth your time?	Does the team meet at the right frequency?	Should you be on this team?	Should this team exist?
	Very Confident Somewhat Confident Not Confident	Definitely Sometimes Usually Not Never	Meets too much Meets often enough Doesn't meet often enough	I'm a good match for this team. I sometimes need to participate and sometimes don't contribute. I don't need to be on this team.	Yes No Yes, but it may need to change somehow I don't know
	Very Confident Somewhat Confident Not Confident	Definitely Sometimes Usually Not Never	Meets too much Meets often enough Doesn't meet often enough	I'm a good match for this team. I sometimes need to participate and sometimes don't contribute. I don't need to be on this team.	Yes No Yes, but it may need to change somehow I don't know

Indicate other teams that you believe you are well-suited to that you are not currently a member of.

A.11: Team Communication Plan

Leadership Team Activity

Team: _____ Date: _____

Level of Urgency	Key Information to Communicate	Audience and Frequency	Person Responsible	Date
This information is: ☐ Nice to Know ☐ Need to Know ☐ Need to Act				
This information is: ☐ Nice to Know ☐ Need to Know ☐ Need to Act				
This information is: ☐ Nice to Know ☐ Need to Know ☐ Need to Act				
This information is: ☐ Nice to Know ☐ Need to Know ☐ Need to Act				
This information is: ☐ Nice to Know ☐ Need to Know ☐ Need to Act				

MTSS for Reading Improvement © 2025 Solution Tree Press • SolutionTree.com

Visit **go.SolutionTree.com/literacy** to download this free reproducible.

A.12: Teams and the Collaborative Improvement Cycle

Leadership Team Activity

Activity

For each of the following activities that teams engage in related to system level reading improvement, identify the team with this responsibility.

Lever for System Change	Do we have a local team that currently addresses this? If so, which team?	If not, is there a current team that is a right match to address this? If so, which team?	Action Needed
Team structures and membership			No action needed Communicate with team Create team
Designing, implementing, and evaluating Tier 1			No action needed Communicate with team Create team
Designing, implementing, and evaluating Tier 2			No action needed Communicate with team Create team
Designing, implementing, and evaluating Tier 3			No action needed Communicate with team Create team
Test or tool selection			No action needed Communicate with team Create team
Assessment / data collection			No action needed Communicate with team Create team
Assessment / data usage			No action needed Communicate with team Create team
Training and coaching on how to use the Collaborative Improvement Cycle			No action needed Communicate with team Create team
Training and coaching on the assessment system			No action needed Communicate with team Create team
Training and coaching on evidence-based reading instruction			No action needed Communicate with team Create team

A.13: Tier 1 Discussion

All-Educator Activity

Overview
The purpose of this activity is to support a building team during an all-educator meeting to reflect on MTSS tiers and consider Tier 1 reading needs.

Activity
Discuss in grade-level teams or in pairs and then open for a large group discussion.

1. What tier do we have the most resources within?
2. Changes in practice in which tier have the highest potential to impact our overall achievement?
3. Which of our Tier 1 practices are consistent across all classrooms within a grade? What varies between classrooms within a grade?
4. What percentage of students who start the year on track do you expect to end the year on track?
5. What questions do you have about Tier 1 and what Tier 1 data would you like to review?

A.14: Allocating Adult Resources

Grade-Level Team and Building Leadership Team Activity

Overview

This activity is designed to help educators think flexibly about using adult resources to improve reading outcomes. The guiding questions prompt reflection on the needs of the students in each grade and the adults who could be available to teach small group interventions in all tiers.

Activity

1. Refer to the Grouping Across the Grade Activity to identify the ideal number of intervention groups needed for this grade.
2. Name the adults who serve students in this grade.
3. Discuss any additional factors that may influence the number of adults who are available to teach small-group intervention for this grade.
4. Think flexibly about the adults who might be available, beyond their typical roles and functions. Consider repurposing related service personnel, paraprofessionals, and so on, and enlisting the support of every adult who has a stake in reading outcomes in this grade.
5. Communicate the adult resources that are needed for Tier 2 and Tier 3 intervention in this grade to the Building Leadership Team and District Leadership Team.

Grade:	
How many groups of students need intervention in this grade?	
List the adults who serve students in this grade. List the names of classroom teachers, related service personnel, special education, reading intervention, and English learner staff at the school, district, and regional agency levels.	
What additional factors should we consider? (for example, personnel who aren't used to working this way, are only in the building on certain days, have an overloaded caseload, the schedule, and so on)	
What are the total number of intervention groups that can be served and who will support each group?	
How will communication be facilitated between the grade-level team and the building leadership team?	

MTSS for Reading Improvement © 2025 Solution Tree Press • SolutionTree.com
Visit **go.SolutionTree.com/literacy** to download this free reproducible.

A.15: Intervention Selection Considerations

Grade-Level Team Activity

Overview

The purpose of this activity is to map out the daily, weekly, and monthly schedule so that sufficient time is available for planning, implementing, and evaluating the Tier 2 and Tier 3 interventions delivered in each grade.

Activity

Discuss the answers to the questions below.

1. Craft the daily, weekly, and monthly schedule related to interventions in this grade.
2. Communicate the needs of this grade level to the building leadership team.

Grade:	
Daily Schedule	
1	How many students need Tier 2 and / or Tier 3 intervention in addition to Tier 1 instruction?
2	When is Tier 1 instruction scheduled?
3	How many minutes are needed for Tier 2?
4	How many minutes are needed for Tier 3?
5	When will instructors collect and review progress monitoring data?
Weekly Schedule	
6	On what day and at what time will each group receive Tier 2 and Tier 3 intervention?
7	When is the weekly grade-level team meeting?
Monthly Schedule	
8	When is the monthly grade-level professional development and coaching meeting?

What needs should be communicated to the building leadership team?

A.16: Intervention Scheduling

Grade-Level Team Activity

Overview

The purpose of this activity is to map out the daily, weekly, and monthly schedule so that sufficient time is available for planning, implementing, and evaluating the Tier 2 and Tier 3 interventions delivered in each grade.

Activity

1. Discuss the answers to the questions below.
2. Craft the intervention schedule.
3. Communicate the needs of this grade level to the building leadership team.

Grade:	
How many students need Tier 2 or Tier 3 intervention in addition to Tier 1 instruction?	
When is Tier 1 instruction scheduled?	
How many minutes are needed for Tier 2 intervention?	
How many minutes are needed for Tier 3 intervention?	
When will progress monitoring data be collected?	
When will teams review progress monitoring data?	

What needs should be communicated to the Building Leadership Team?

A.17: Comparing Intensity

All-Educator Meeting

Purpose: The purpose of this activity is to allow all educators in a building to consider how intervention intensity impacts student growth.

Use: Discuss at grade-level teams or at tables and then engage in large group discussion.

Discussion

How do we set goals for students in interventions? Do we differentiate the growth we expect by the intensity of our intervention?

Go to your intervention program materials. Let's see what happens to student skill acquisition with different levels of intensity of the same 8-week intervention. What skills are students learning after 8 weeks if we are able to complete 2, 3, 4, or 5 lessons a week in that program?

2 lessons a week (lesson 16)	3 lessons a week (lesson 24)	4 lessons a week (lesson 32)	5 lessons a week (lesson 40)

What do you notice? Do you think that increasing the intensity of interventions or ensuring that you're able to complete more lessons each week will result in greater student growth?

A.18: MTSS World Café

All-Educator Activity

Purpose: Reflect on key learnings and celebrate reading improvement within an MTSS.

Directions

1. Put a large sticky note and markers on each table during an all-educator meeting.
2. Provide each table with one of the following prompts. Note that each table will have a different prompt to add to their large sticky note.
    a. What were the most important insights you gained from the book that had an impact on your everyday practice?
    b. How have your data use practices changed since we've engaged in this work?
    c. How can we involve families and the wider community in our MTSS efforts related to reading improvement?
    d. What is the next thing you're excited to implement as a result of our current work and the book?
    e. Has your collaboration changed? If so, in what ways?
    f. What role should our Building Leadership Team play in supporting future improvement efforts?
    g. How do you see the things we've learned applying to our students who are accelerated learners, those with disabilities, and our multilingual learners?
3. Have each table discuss and add their ideas to their sticky note.
4. Put all sticky notes on the wall in various parts of the room.
5. Have teams shift to another note, read the question and current responses, and add to them.
6. Continue shifting until each team has been at each note.
7. Debrief as a large group.

APPENDIX B

MTSS Meeting Guide

B.1: Grade-Level Team Agenda Tier 1

Team Roles

Role	Today's Talent
Facilitator	
Timekeeper	
Note Taker	
Discussion Leader	

Gap Identification	Gap Analysis	Action Planning

Agenda

Topic	Task	Time	Notes
Agenda Review	Who will complete each of the team roles today?		
Tier 1 Gap Identification	Is Tier 1 implementation effective for students in our grade?		
Tier 1 Gap Identification	Is our Tier 1 instruction equitable?		
Tier 1 Gap Identification	Does our Tier 1 instruction result in too many students being identified as having a specific learning disability?		

MTSS for Reading Improvement © 2025 Solution Tree Press • SolutionTree.com
Visit **go.SolutionTree.com/literacy** to download this free reproducible.

Topic	Task	Time	Notes
Tier 1 Gap Identification	What is our gap identification summary statement?		
Tier 1 Gap Analysis	What needs and resources did we identify?		
Tier 1 Gap Analysis	What are our prioritized needs?		
Tier 1 Gap Analysis	What are our existing strengths and resource needs?		
Tier 1 Action Planning	What will we do to support our students?		
Closing	What are our next steps?		

Follow-Up

Task	Talent	Timeline

MTSS for Reading Improvement © 2025 Solution Tree Press • SolutionTree.com
Visit **go.SolutionTree.com/literacy** to download this free reproducible.

B.2: Grade-Level Team Protocol Tier 1 Gap Identification

Purpose: Identify the extent to which our Tier 1 resources are effective and equitable.

School	
Grade	
Screening Period	
Team Members	

Part 1: Is Tier 1 implementation effective for students in our grade?

Team Questions	Answers
What percent of students are on track at the grade level in each skill area? (Leave blank if your screening tool doesn't give a score for a specific reading domain.)	
• Phonemic Awareness	
• Phonics	
• Fluency	
• Comprehension	
• Broad Reading/Composite	
On the Broad Reading/Composite measure, what percent of students who started the year on track are still on track?	

Effective Tier 1 implementation typically results in at least 80 percent of students meeting targets in all areas and 95 percent or more of students who start the year on track continuing on track.

Part 2: Is our Tier 1 instruction equitable?

Group	Percent Meeting Screening Target
American Indian or Alaska Native	
Black or African American	
Hispanic or Latino of Any Race	
White	
Asian	
Native Hawaiian or Other Pacific Islander	
Not Receiving Free-Reduced Lunch	
Receiving Free-Reduced Lunch	
Students not Receiving English Learning Services	
Multilingual students receiving English Learning Services	
Did all students who needed intervention receive it?	

Part 3: Does our Tier 1 instruction result in too many students being identified as having a specific learning disability?

	Grade Level	State Average
What percent of students are identified with a specific learning disability?		

Gap-Identification Summary Statement or Statements (Complete at least one.)

Our Tier 1 is effective and equitable.

Our Tier 1 is effective for some students but is not equitable for all groups. Specifically, there is a _____% gap in outcomes for students who are _____ and those who are _____.

Our Tier 1 is not effective. We expect _____% of students to meet screening benchmarks. _____% of students in _____ grade are meeting screening targets.

Other:

Next Step: Use the Tier 1 Gap Analysis Protocol to analyze factors contributing to identified universal system gaps.

B.3: Grade-Level Team Protocol Tier 1 Gap Analysis

Purpose: Identify specific needs within Tier 1 reading instruction.

School	
Grade	
Screening Period	
Team Members	

For those areas with fewer than 80 percent of students meeting screening targets, consider each of the potential areas of need.

System Lever for Change	Questions to Consider	Answers and Data	Perceived Need
Strategic Leadership and Teaming	• Do we have the right team members on strategic leadership teams and grade-level teams to ensure needed expertise, perspective, and consensus? • Do teams have regular time to address reading needs and act on reading data?		
Collaborative Improvement Cycle	• Do strategic leadership teams and grade-level teams use data protocols that guide their use of the Collaborative Improvement Cycle? • Do teams have experts in the Collaborative Improvement Cycle supporting their data use?		
Effective and Equitable Tiered Supports	• Are we able to spend at least 90–120 minutes in reading instruction daily? • Do we have a clear scope and sequence for teaching foundational reading skills? • Are we on track to finish all lessons this year? • Are instructional strategies clear and evidence-based?		
Impactful Assessment System	• Do grade-level teams have access to screening data and protocols to support use of those data? • Do we use formative assessment to inform our daily instruction? • Do strategic leadership teams have data protocols to support use of schoolwide reading data?		

System Lever for Change	Questions to Consider	Answers and Data	Perceived Need
Targeted Professional Learning	• Have all grade-level teachers been trained in, and feel confident around, evidence-based instruction aligned with the reading science? • Have all grade-level teachers been trained in, and feel confident in, using our curricular materials? • Do all educators have access to coaching resources to drive improved reading outcomes?		

Prioritize identified needs. Consider both local data and those actions that are feasible and expected to make the biggest impact on student reading growth.

Top Priority: _____

Second Priority: _____

Outline Existing Strengths and Resources. Identify those resources that can be used to address prioritized needs.

Next Steps. We expect that if we address _____

and _____, our Tier 1 will become

more effective and/or equitable.

B.4: Grade-Level Team Action Plan

Purpose: Decide and document next steps based on gap analysis and identify resources needed to improve our success.

Action Item	Who will ensure this action gets completed?	When will we implement this action?	How will we monitor that it is able to be implemented?

What data will we use to determine if this plan is effective?

When will we evaluate the effects of our plan?

What additional support does the grade-level team need from the building leadership team to implement the action plan?

MTSS for Reading Improvement © 2025 Solution Tree Press • SolutionTree.com
Visit **go.SolutionTree.com/literacy** to download this free reproducible.

B.5: Building Leadership Team Agenda

Team Roles

Role	Today's Talent
Facilitator	
Timekeeper	
Note Taker	
Discussion Leader	

Gap Identification	Gap Analysis	Action Planning

Agenda

Topic	Task	Time	Notes
Agenda Review	Who will complete each of the team roles today?		
Gap Identification	Is our reading instruction effective and equitable? If not, at which grade levels do we have needs?		
Gap Identification	Are students growing adequately and equitably?		
Gap Identification	Does our instruction and intervention result in too many students being identified as having a specific learning disability?		
Gap Identification	What is our gap identification summary statement?		

Topic	Task	Time	Notes
Gap Analysis	What did grade-level teams identify as priorities for action?		
Gap Analysis	How should we allocate school-level resources to address needs in: • Strategic Leadership and Teaming • Collaborative Improvement Cycle • Effective and Equitable Tiered Supports • Impactful Assessment System • Targeted Professional Learning		
Action Planning	What will we do to support our grade-level teams?		
Action Planning	What do we need to communicate with grade-level teams and with the district leadership team?		
Closing	What are our next steps?		

Follow-Up

Task	Talent	Timeline

B.6: Building Leadership Team Protocol Gap Identification

Purpose: Identify the extent to which our reading MTSS system is effective and equitable.

Student Reading Data

Is our reading instruction effective and equitable? If not, at which grade levels do we have needs?

Team Questions	Grade Level						
Tier 1 What percent of students meet screening targets on the Broad Reading/Composite measure?							
Tiers 2 and 3 What percent of students who receive intervention, including students receiving SDI, meet screening targets on the Broad Reading/Composite measure?							
Analyze data by student group. Which student group gaps are found?							

Reading Growth (middle of year and end of year)

Are students growing adequately and equitably?

Team Questions	Grade Level						
Tier 1 On the Broad Reading/Composite measure, what percent of students who started the year on track are still on track?							
Tiers 2 and 3 On the Broad Reading/Composite measure, what percent of students who received intervention are on track to meet their goals?							
Analyze data by student group. Which student group gaps are found?							

Does our instruction and intervention result in too many students being identified as having a specific learning disability?

Team Questions	Grade Level						
What percent of students are identified with a specific learning disability?							
What is the state average?							

Summary Statement or Statements (complete at least one)

Our instruction and intervention is effective and equitable at each grade level.

For which grade(s) and tier(s) are instruction and intervention systems effective for some students but not equitable for all groups? Specifically, there is a _____% gap in outcomes for students who are _____ _____

and those who are _____ in grade _____.

Our instruction and intervention are potentially resulting in an overidentification of students who have specific learning disabilities, based on a higher-than average identification rate.

Other:

B.7: Building Leadership Team Protocol Gap Analysis

Purpose: Identify why instruction and interventions are not effective and/or equitable.

What areas of need did each grade-level team prioritize? What patterns do you notice?

	Grade							
Strategic Leadership and Teaming								
Collaborative Improvement Cycle								
Effective and Equitable Tiered Supports								
Impactful Assessment System								
Targeted Professional Learning								

What needs did each grade-level team request?

Grade	Needs From Building Leadership Team

B.8: Building Leadership Team Action Plan

Purpose: Decide and document next steps and support for grade-level teams based on their gap analysis and your data review.

Grade	Gap Analysis Summary	Action Item	Lead

When will we evaluate the effects of our plan?

What information needs to be communicated to grade-level teams? To the district leadership team?

MTSS for Reading Improvement © 2025 Solution Tree Press • SolutionTree.com
Visit **go.SolutionTree.com/literacy** to download this free reproducible.

B.9: Grade-Level Team Agenda Tiers 2 and 3

Team Roles

Role	Today's Talent
Facilitator	
Timekeeper	
Note Taker	
Discussion Leader	

Gap Identification	Gap Analysis	Action Planning

Agenda

Topic	Task	Time	Notes
Agenda Review	Who will complete each of the team roles today?		
Tiers 2 and 3 Gap Identification	Is implementation of Tier 2 and 3 intervention effective for students in our grade?		
Tiers 2 and 3 Gap Identification	Are our Tier 2 and 3 intervention systems equitable?		
Tiers 2 and 3 Gap Identification	Do our Tier 2 and 3 interventions result in too many students being identified as having a Specific Learning Disability or dyslexia?		
Tiers 2 and 3 Gap Identification	What is our gap identification summary statement?		
Tiers 2 and 3 Gap Analysis	What needs and resources did we identify?		

Topic	Task	Time	Notes
Tiers 2 and 3 Gap Analysis	What are our prioritized needs?		
Tiers 2 and 3 Gap Analysis	What are our existing strengths and resource needs?		
Tiers 2 and 3 Action Planning	What will we do to support our students?		
Closing	What are our next steps?		

Follow-Up

Task	Talent	Timeline

B.10: Grade-Level Team Protocol Tiers 2 and 3 Gap Identification

Purpose: Analyze the effectiveness of Tier 2 and Tier 3 reading interventions.

School	
Grade	
Screening Period	
Team Members	

Part 1: Is our current intervention system effective for students in our grade?

Team Questions	Answers
What percent of students who receive intervention are on track at the grade level in each skill area?	
• Phonemic Awareness	
• Phonics	
• Fluency	
• Comprehension	
• Broad Reading/Composite	

Effective intervention systems typically result in at least 80 percent of students who receive them to make sufficient progress.

Part 2: Are current interventions effective for students they serve?

Intervention	Percent with minimal growth	Percent making some growth but not on track to meet goal	Percent on track to meet goal

If most students in an intervention group aren't on track to meet their goal, go to gap analysis.

Gap Identification Summary Statement or Statements (choose at least one)

Our intervention system is effective for all.

We expect our intervention system to cause at least 80% of the students who receive intervention to be on track toward their goals but only _____ percent of _____ students are making progress.

Some interventions are effective, but these are resulting in insufficient growth: _____
_____

Other:

Next Step: Use the Gap Analysis Protocol to analyze factors contributing to identified intervention system gaps.

B.11: Grade-Level Team Tier 2 and 3 Gap Analysis

Purpose: Identify specific needs within Tier 2 and Tier 3 reading intervention.

School	
Grade	
Screening Period	
Team Members	

For those interventions with fewer than 80 percent of students on track to meet their goals, consider each of the potential areas of need.

System Lever for Change	Questions to Consider	Answers and Data	Perceived Need
Strategic Leadership and Teaming	• Does the school leadership team provide adequate time in the schedule for planning, implementing, and evaluating reading interventions? • Does the school leadership team allocate resources for adequate personnel to deliver necessary interventions?		
Collaborative Improvement Cycle	• Are data used by grade-level teams to design Tier 2 and Tier 3 interventions? • Are data used by student-level teams to intensify Tier 3 interventions?		

page 1 of 2

System Lever for Change	Questions to Consider	Answers and Data	Perceived Need
Effective and Equitable Tiered Supports	• Are research-aligned intervention programs available that match the needs of students? • Are interventions targeted to the lowest skill in the sequence that the student needs to learn? • Are students with the greatest skill gaps in the smallest intervention groups? • Are we able to spend at least 30 minutes 3–5 times per week for Tier 2 interventions and 45–60 minutes per day in Tier 3 interventions? • Are interventions provided in addition to Tier 1? • Are instructional strategies evidence-based? • Do we use data to guide intervention intensification when students do not make sufficient progress?		
Impactful Assessment System	• Are screening and diagnostic data used to identify the intervention needs of students? • Are screening and progress monitoring data used to evaluate the effectiveness of interventions? • Are diagnostic and progress monitoring data used to intensify interventions as needed?		
Targeted Professional Learning	• Have all educators been trained in, and feel confident around, evidence-based instruction aligned with the science of reading? • Have all educators received timely training in, and feel confident using, interventions they'll deliver?		

Prioritize identified needs. Consider both local data and those actions that are feasible and expected to make the biggest impact on student reading growth.

Top Priority: _____

Second Priority: _____

Outline Existing Strengths and Resources. Identify those resources that can be used to address prioritized needs.

Next Steps. We expect that if we address _____ and _____

we _____

B.12: Grade-Level Team Agenda Outcome Analysis

Team Roles

Role	Today's Talent
Facilitator	
Timekeeper	
Note Taker	
Discussion Leader	

Outcome Analysis	Gap Analysis	Action Planning

Agenda

Topic	Task	Time	Notes
Agenda Review	Who will complete each of the team roles today?		
Outcome Analysis	What were our summary gap identification statements?		
Outcome Analysis	What is our current reading achievement?		
Outcome Analysis	How have we implemented our action plans?		
Outcome Analysis	What are our student outcomes?		
Gap Analysis	What are next priorities for improvement?		

MTSS for Reading Improvement © 2025 Solution Tree Press • SolutionTree.com

Visit **go.SolutionTree.com/literacy** to download this free reproducible.

Topic	Task	Time	Notes
Action Planning	What do we need to do to support our students?		
Closing	What are our next steps?		

Follow-Up

Task	Talent	Timeline

B.13: Building Leadership Team Agenda Outcome Analysis

Team Roles

Role	Today's Talent
Facilitator	
Timekeeper	
Note Taker	
Discussion Leader	

Outcome Analysis	Gap Analysis	Action Planning

Agenda

Topic	Task	Time	Notes
Agenda Review	Who will complete each of the team roles today?		
Outcome Analysis	What were our summary gap identification statements?		
Outcome Analysis	What is our current reading achievement?		
Outcome Analysis	How have we implemented our action plans?		
Outcome Analysis	What are our student outcomes?		
Gap Analysis	What are next priorities for improvement?		

Topic	Task	Time	Notes
Action Planning	What do we need to do to support our grade-level teams?		
Closing	What are our next steps?		

Follow-Up

Task	Talent	Timeline

B.14: Grade-Level Team Protocol Outcome Analysis

Purpose: Evaluate the extent to which our action plan was effective and equitable.
What was your initial summary statement or statements?

Student Reading Data

Team Questions	Answers
What is the change in percentage of students who meet screening targets?	
• Phonemic Awareness	
• Phonics	
• Fluency	
• Comprehension	
• Broad Reading/Composite	
On the Broad Reading/Composite measure, what percent of students who started the year on track are still on track?	
Analyze data by student group. Did any student group not make as much growth as the entire grade level?	
What percentage of students who received intervention are on track to meet their goals?	

Action Plan Implementation

Team Questions	Answers
What parts were you able to successfully implement?	
For those actions the team was unable to complete, what were the barriers to implementing them as expected?	

Analysis Summary

<table>
<tr><th rowspan="2"></th><th colspan="3">Student Growth</th></tr>
<tr><th colspan="2">We had low levels of student growth and/or student group gaps.</th><th>We had high levels of student growth and no student group gaps.</th></tr>
<tr><td rowspan="2">Action Plan Implementation</td><td>We couldn't implement many parts of the plan.</td><td>Revisit the plan and request support to remove any barriers to implementation.</td><td>Reflect on the actions the team took to achieve this success.</td></tr>
<tr><td>We were able to implement most, if not all, of the plan.</td><td>Revisit gap analysis and improve action plan.</td><td>Reflect on the actions the team took to achieve this success.</td></tr>
</table>

What additional support do you need from the Building Leadership team?

B.15: Building Leadership Team Protocol Outcome Analysis

Purpose: Identify the extent to which our action plans were effective and equitable.

Student Reading Data

	Grade Level						
What percentage of students met growth targets?							
On the Broad Reading/Composite measure, what percent of students who started the year on track are still on track?							
On the Broad Reading/Composite measure, what percent of students who received intervention are on track to meet their goals?							
Analyze data by student group. Did any student group make less growth than the entire grade level?							

Action Plan Implementation

Team Questions	Answers
What parts were you able to successfully implement?	
For those actions the team was unable to complete, what were the barriers to implementing them as expected?	

Analysis Summary

	Student Growth	
	We had low levels of student growth and/or student group gaps.	**We had high levels of student growth and no student group gaps.**
Action Plan Implementation	We weren't able to implement many parts of the plan.	Revisit the plan and provide support to remove any barriers to implementation.	Reflect on the actions the team took to achieve this success.
	We were able to implement most, if not all, of the plan.	Revisit gap analysis and improve action plan.	Reflect on the actions the team took to achieve this success.

What information needs to be communicated to grade-level teams? To the District Leadership Team?

B.16: Team Growth Reflection

Grade-Level Team Activity

Discussion
Where did we see improved student growth? • Tier 1 • Tier 2 • Tier 3 What did we address in our Action Plan related to those tiers?   What did we do differently to support students in reading in that Tier?   How do you think it impacted their growth?   Will you continue the practice? Why or why not?

References

95 Percent Group. (2024). *95 Phonics Core Program® Grade 1 Teacher's Edition Set of 3 Volumes*. 95 Percent Group Inc.

Adams, C. M., & Forsyth, P. B. (2006). Proximate sources of collective teacher efficacy. *Journal of Educational Administration, 44*(6), 625–642. https://doi.org/10.1108/09578230610704828

Al Otaiba, S., Connor, C. M., Folsom, J. S., Greulich, L., Meadows, J., & Li, Z. (2011). Assessment data—Informed guidance to individualize kindergarten reading instruction: Findings from a cluster-randomized control field trial. *The Elementary School Journal, 111*(4), 535–560. https://doi.org/10.1086/659031

Al Otaiba, S., & Fuchs, D. (2006). Who are the young children for whom best practices in reading are ineffective? An experimental and longitudinal study. *Journal of Learning Disabilities, 39*(5), 414–431. https://doi.org/10.1177/00222194060390050401

Archer, A. L., & Hughes, C. A. (2011). *Explicit instruction: Effective and efficient teaching*. New York: Guilford Press.

Australian Children's Education and Care Quality Authority (n.d.). *National quality framework*. Accessed at https://www.acecqa.gov.au/national-quality-framework on August 2, 2024.

Bandura, A. (1993). Perceived self-efficacy in cognitive development and functioning. *Educational Psychologist, 28*(2), 117–148. https://doi.org/10.1207/s15326985ep2802_3

Batsche, G. M., Elliott, J., Graden, J. L., Grimes, J., Kovaleski, J. F., Prasse, D., et al. (2006). *Response to intervention: Policy considerations and implementation*. Alexandria, VA: National Association of State Directors of Special Education. Accessed at https://cdnsm5-ss9.sharpschool.com/UserFiles/Servers/Server_360846/File/Academics/Curriculum%20&%20Instruction/RTI/Powerpoint%20from%20IDEA%20Partnership.pdf on August 2, 2024.

Blachman, B. A. (1995, March). *Identifying the core linguistic deficits and the critical conditions for early intervention with children with reading disabilities* [Conference presentation]. Learning Disabilities Association 2017 Annual Meeting, Orlando, FL.

Brown, B. (2018). *Dare to lead: Brave work, tough conversations, whole hearts*. New York: Random House

California Reading Coalition. (n.d.). *Reading program listings*. Accessed at https://www.careads.org/curric-list on August 2, 2024.

Cárdenas-Hagan, E. (2020). *Literacy foundations for English learners: A comprehensive guide to evidence-based instruction*. Baltimore, MD: Paul Brookes.

Carnine, D. (1999). Campaigns for moving research into practice. *Remedial and Special Education, 20*(1), 2–35. https://doi.org/10.1177/074193259902000101

Carnine, D. W., Silbert, J., Kame'enui, E. J., Tarver, S. G., & Jungjuhann, K. (2006). *Teaching struggling and at-risk readers: A direct instruction approach*. Upper Saddle River, NJ: Pearson.

Castles, A., Rastle, K., & Nation, K. (2018). Ending the reading wars: Reading acquisition from novice to expert. *Psychological Science in the Public Interest, 19*(1), 5–51. https://doi.org/10.1177/1529100618772271

Chen, O., Castro-Alonso, J. C., Paas, F., & Sweller, J. (2018). Extending cognitive load theory to incorporate working memory resource depletion: Evidence from the spacing effect. *Educational Psychology Review, 30*(2), 483–501. https://doi.org/10.1007/s10648-017-9426-2

Cheryan, S., Ziegler, S. A., Plaut, V. C., & Meltzoff, A. N. (2014). Designing classrooms to maximize student achievement. *Policy Insights from the Behavioral and Brain Sciences, 1*(1), 4–12. https://doi.org/10.1177/2372732214548677

Clark, R. E., Kirschner, P. A., & Sweller, J. (2012). Putting students on the path to learning: The case for fully guided instruction. *American Educator, 36*(1), 6–11.

Clemens, N. H., Hagan-Burke, S., Luo, W., Cerda, C., Blakely, A., Frosch, J., et al. (2015). The predictive validity of a computer-adaptive assessment of kindergarten and first-grade reading skills. *School Psychology Review, 44*(1), 76–97. https://doi.org/10.17105/spr44-1.76-97

Clemens, N. H., Lai, M. H. C., Burke, M., & Wu, J.-Y. (2017). Interrelations of growth in letter naming and sound fluency in kindergarten and implications for subsequent reading fluency. *School Psychology Review, 46*(3), 272–287. https://doi.org/10.17105/spr-2017-0032.v46-3

Curtis, M. J., & Stollar, S. A. (2002). Best practices in system-level change. In A. Thomas & J. Grimes (Eds.), *Best practices in school psychology IV* (pp. 223–234). Bethesda, MD: National Association of School Psychologists.

Dehaene, S. (2009). *Reading in the brain: The new science of how we read*. New York: Penguin Books.

Deno, S. L. (1989). Curriculum-based measurement and special education services: A fundamental and direct relationship. In M. R. Shinn (Ed.), *Curriculum-based measurement: Assessing special children* (pp. 1–17). New York: Guilford Press.

Deno, S. L. (2016). Data-based decision-making. In S. R. Jimerson, M. K. Burns, & A. M. VanDerHeyden (Eds.), *Handbook of response to intervention: The science and practice of multi-tiered systems of support* (2nd ed., pp. 9–28). Springer Science + Business Media.

Donohoo, J., Hattie, J., & Eells, R. (2018). The power of collective efficacy. *Educational Leadership, 75*(6), 40–44.

Doty, S. J., Hixson, M. D., Decker, D. M., Reynolds, J. L., & Drevon, D. D. (2015). Reliability and validity of advanced phonics measures. *Journal of Psychoeducational Assessment, 33*, 503–521. https://doi.org/10.1177/0734282914567870

DuFour, R., DuFour, R., Eaker, R., Many, T. W., Mattos, M., & Muhammad, A. (2024). *Learning by doing: A handbook for professional learning communities at work* (4th ed.). Bloomington, IN: Solution Tree Press.

Duncan, A., & Brown, S. (2024, June 26). *What's possible in a year? One school's growth using FastBridge to Drive SoR instruction & intervention* [Conference presentation]. Iowa Reading Association's Annual Conference.

Eells, R. J. (2011). *Meta-analysis of the relationship between collective teacher efficacy and student achievement* [Doctoral dissertation, Loyola University Chicago]. Loyola eCommons. Accessed at https://ecommons.luc.edu/luc_diss/133 on January 12, 2025.

Ehri, L. C. (2020). The science of learning to read words: A case for systematic phonics instruction. *Reading Research Quarterly, 55*(S1), S45–S60.

Ervin, R. A., Schaughency, E., Goodman, S. D., McGlinchey, M. T., & Matthews, A. (2006). Merging research and practice agendas to address reading and behavior school-wide. *School Psychology Review, 35*(2), 198–223. https://doi.org/10.1080/02796015.2006.12087987

Feldman, K. (2018, June 25). *Literate student engagement: Every classroom, every lesson, every day!* [Conference session]. BEST/MTSS Summer Institute, Killington, VT. Accessed at https://www.pbisvermont.org/wp-content/uploads/2018/06/VT-Engagement-2018-POST-2.0.pdf on August 2, 2024.

Filderman, M. J., Toste, J. R., Didion, L. A., Peng, P., & Clemens, N. H. (2018). Data-based decision making in reading interventions: A synthesis and meta-analysis of the effects for struggling readers. *The Journal of Special Education, 52*(3), 174–187.

Fixsen, D. L., Blasé, K. A., & Van Dyke, M. K. (2019). *Implementation practice and science*. Chapel Hill, NC: Active Implementation Research Network.

Foorman B., Beyler N., Borradaile K., Coyne M., Denton C., Dimino J., et al. (2016). *Foundational skills to support reading for understanding in kindergarten through 3rd grade* (NCEE 2016–4008). Washington, DC: National Center for Education Evaluation and Regional Assistance (NCEE), Institute of Education Sciences, U. S. Department of Education. Accessed at https://ies.ed.gov/ncee/wwc/Docs/PracticeGuide/wwc_foundationalreading_070516.pdf on August 2, 2024.

Foster-Fishman, P. G., Nowell, B., & Yang, H. (2007). Putting the system back into systems change: A framework for understanding and changing organizational and community systems. *American Journal of Community Psychology, 39*(3–4), 197–215. https://doi.org/.10.1007/s10464-007-9109-0

Francis, D. J., Shaywitz, S. E., Stuebing, K. K., Shaywitz, B. A., & Fletcher, J. M. (1996). Developmental lag versus deficit models of reading disability: A longitudinal, individual growth curves analysis. *Journal of Educational Psychology, 88*(1), 3–17. https://doi.org/10.1037/0022-0663.88.1.3

Fuchs, L. S., Fuchs, D., Hamlett, C. L., & Stecker, P. M. (2021). Bringing data-based individualization to scale: A call for the next-generation technology of teacher supports. *Journal of Learning Disabilities, 54*(5), 319–333.

Fuchs, L. S., Fuchs, D., Hosp, M., & Jenkins, J. (2001). Oral reading fluency as an indicator of reading competence: A theoretical, empirical, and historical analysis. *Scientific Studies of Reading, 5*(3), 239–256. https://doi.org/10.1207/S1532799XSSR0503_3

Fuchs, L. S., Fuchs, D., & Malone, A. S. (2017). The taxonomy of intervention intensity. *TEACHING Exceptional Children, 50*(1), 35–43. https://doi.org/10.1177/0040059917703962

Gibbons, K., Brown, S., & Niebling, B. C. (2019). *Effective universal instruction: An action-oriented approach to improving Tier 1*. New York: Guilford Press.

Good, R. H., III, Kaminski, R. A., Cummings, K., Dufour-Martel, C., Petersen, K., Powell-Smith, K., et al. (2011, revised 2018). *Acadience Reading K–6*. Eugene, OR: Acadience Learning. Accessed at https://acadiencelearning.org on January 12, 2025. (Original work published as DIBELS Next).

Goos, M., Pipa, J., & Peixoto, F. (2021). Effectiveness of grade retention: A systematic review and meta-analysis. *Educational Research Review, 34*, 1–14. https://doi.org/10.1016/j.edurev.2021.100401

Gough, P. B., & Tunmer, W. E. (1986). Decoding, reading, and reading disability. *Remedial and Special Education, 7*(1), 6–10. https://doi.org/10.1177/074193258600700104

Graden, J. L., Stollar, S. A., & Poth, R. L. (2007). The Ohio Integrated Systems Model: Overview and lessons learned. In S. R. Jimerson, M. K. Burns, & A. M. VanDerHeyden (Eds.), *Handbook of response to intervention: The science and practice of assessment and intervention* (pp. 288–299). New York: Springer Science + Business Media.

Graden, J. L., Zins, J. E., & Curtis, M. J. (1988). *Alternative educational delivery systems: Enhancing instructional options for all students*. Bethesda, MD: National Association of School Psychologists.

Gresham, F. M. (1989). Assessment of treatment integrity in school consultation and prereferral intervention. *School Psychology Review, 18*(1), 37–50. https://doi.org/10.1080/02796015.1989.12085399

Grissom, J. A., Egalite, A. J., & Lindsay, C. A. (2021). *How principals affect students and schools: A systematic synthesis of two decades of research.* The Wallace Foundation. Accessed at www.wallacefoundation.org/knowledge-center/Documents/How-Principals-Affect-Students-and-Schools.pdf on January 10, 2025.

Hamman, J. (Host). (2019, December 2). Unpacking progress: What it takes to raise school literacy rates (No. 3) [Audio podcast episode]. In *Ed Leaders in Literacy.* Accessed at www.gleaneducation.com/ed-leaders-podcast/principal-sharon-dunn on December 20. 2024.

Haring, N. G., & Eaton, M. D. (1978). Systematic procedures: An instructional hierarchy. In N. G. Haring, T. C. Lovitt, M. D. Eaton, & C. L. Hansen, (Eds.), *The fourth R: Research in the classroom.* Columbus, OH: C. E. Merrill.

Harn, B. A., Chard, D. J., & Kame'enui, E. J. (2011). Meeting societies' increased expectations through responsive instruction: The power and potential of systemwide approaches. *Preventing School Failure: Alternative Education for Children and Youth, 55*(4), 232–239. https://doi.org/10.1080/1045988X.2010.548416

Heller, K. A., Holtzman, W. H., & Messick, S. J. (1982). *Placing children in special education: a strategy for equity.* Washington, DC: National Academy Press. Accessed at https://nap.nationalacademies.org/read/9440/chapter/1 on August 2, 2024.

Helman, L., & Rosheim, K. (2016). The role of professional learning communities in successful response to intervention implementation. In S. R. Jimerson, M. K. Burns, & A. M. VanDerHeyden (Eds.), *Handbook of Response to Intervention: The science and practice of multi-tiered systems of support* (2nd ed., pp. 89–102). New York: Springer Science + Business Media.

Hoover, W. A., & Gough, P. B. (1990). The simple view of reading. *Reading and Writing, 2*(2), 127–160. https://doi.org/10.1007/bf00401799

Hoover, W. A., & Tunmer, W. E. (2018). The simple view of reading: Three assessments of its adequacy. *Remedial and Special Education, 39*(5), 304–312.

Hoover, W. A., & Tunmer, W. E. (2022). The primacy of science in communicating advances in the science of reading. *Reading Research Quarterly, 57*(2), 399–408. https://doi.org/10.1002/rrq.446

Hosp, M. K., & Fuchs, L. S. (2005). Using CBM as an indicator of decoding, word reading, and comprehension: Do the relations change with grade? *School Psychology Review, 34*(1), 9–26. https://doi.org/10.1080/02796015.2005.12086272

Hosp, M. K., Hosp, J. L., Howell, K. W., & Allison, R. (2014). *The ABCs of curriculum-based evaluation: A practical guide to effective decision making.* New York: Guilford Press.

Jimerson, S. R. (2001). Meta-analysis of grade retention research: Implications for practice in the 21st century. *School Psychology Review, 30*(3), 420–437. https://doi.org/10.1080/02796015.2001.12086124

Jimerson, S. R., Burns, M. K., & VanDerHeyden, A. (Eds.). (2016). *Handbook of response to intervention: The science and practice of assessment and intervention.* New York: Springer Science + Business Media.

Johnston, J., Knight, M., & Miller, L. (2007). Finding time for teams: Student achievement grows as district support boosts collaboration. *Journal of Staff Development, 28*(2), 14–18.

Juel, C. (1988). Learning to read and write: A longitudinal study of 54 children from first through fourth grades. *Journal of Educational Psychology, 80*(4), 437–447. https://doi.org/10.1037/0022-0663.80.4.437

Kame'enui, E. J., & Simmons, D. C. (1999). *Toward successful inclusion of students with disabilities: the architecture of instruction: An overview of materials adaptations.* Reston, VA: Council for Exceptional Children. Accessed at https://files.eric.ed.gov/fulltext/ED429381.pdf on August 2, 2024.

Kame'enui, E. J., Simmons, D. C., & Coyne, M. D. (2000). Schools as host environments: Toward a schoolwide reading improvement model. *Annals of Dyslexia, 50*, 31–51. https://doi.org/10.1007/s11881-000-0016-4

Kearns, D. M., & Fuchs, D. (2013). Does cognitively focused instruction improve the academic performance of low-achieving students? *Exceptional Children, 79*(3), 263–290. https://doi.org/10.1177/001440291307900200

Kellam, S. G., Mackenzie, A. C. L., Brown, C. H., Poduska, J. M., Wang, W., Petras, H., et al. (2011). The good behavior game and the future of prevention and treatment. *Addiction Science & Clinical Practice, 6*(1), 73–84.

Kirschner, P. A., Sweller, J., & Clark, R. E. (2006). Why minimal guidance during instruction does not work: An analysis of the failure of constructivist, discovery, problem-based, experiential, and inquiry-based teaching. *Educational Psychologist, 41*(2), 75–86. https://doi.org/10.1207/s15326985ep4102_1

Klauda, S. L., & Guthrie, J. T. (2008). Relationships of three components of reading fluency to reading comprehension. *Journal of Educational Psychology, 100*(2), 310–321. https://doi.org/10.1037/0022-0663.100.2.310

Lewis, C. (2015). What is improvement science? Do we need it in education? *Educational Researcher, 44*(1), 54–61. https://doi.org/10.3102/0013189×15570388

Lucariello, J., Graham, S., Nastasi, B., Dwyer, C., Skiba, R., Plucker, J., et al. (2015). *Top 20 principles from psychology for preK–12 teaching and learning.* Washington, DC: American Psychological Association. Accessed at http://www.apa.org/ed/schools/cpse/top-twenty-principles.pdf on August 2, 2024.

Martin, N., & McLarren, M. (2023, October 5). What reading curriculum did your district use last year? Look it up here. *The Boston Globe.* Accessed at https://www.bostonglobe.com/2023/10/05/metro/massachusetts-science-of-reading-curriculum-balanced-literacy August 2, 2024.

Marzano, R. J., Waters, T., & McNulty, B. A. (2005). *School leadership that works: From research to results.* Arlington, VA: ASCD.

Mayer, R. E. (2004). Should there be a three-strikes rule against pure discovery learning? *American Psychologist, 59*(1), 14–19. https://doi.org/10.1037/0003-066X.59.1.14

McIntosh, K., & Goodman, S. (2016). *Integrated multi-tiered systems of support: Blending RTI and PBIS.* New York: Guilford Press.

McLaughlin, M. W. (1990). The Rand Change Agent study revisited: Macro perspectives and micro realities. *Educational Researcher, 19*(9), 11–16. https://doi.org/10.3102/0013189X019009011

Meadows Center (2016). *Sample literacy blocks, K–5.* Texas Education Agency. Accessed at https://meadowscenter.org/wp-content/uploads/2022/04/Reading_Blocks1.pdf on August 2, 2024.

Moreno, R. (2004). Decreasing cognitive load for novice students: Effects of explanatory versus corrective feedback in discovery-based multimedia. *Instructional Science, 32,* 99–113. https://doi.org/10.1023/B:TRUC.0000021811.66966.1d

Murphy, J. (2004). Leadership for literacy: A framework for policy and practice. *School Effectiveness and School Improvement, 15*(1), 65–96. https://doi.org/10.1076/sesi.15.1.65.27495

National Association for the Education of Young Children. (2020). *Developmentally appropriate practice.* Accessed at https://www.naeyc.org/resources/developmentally-appropriate-practice on August 2, 2024.

National Association of School Psychologists. (1986). *Rights without labels: A position statement.* Adopted by the Executive Board/Delegate Assembly of the National Association of School Psychologists.

National Center on Intensive Intervention. (2021). *Academic screening tools chart.* Accessed at https://charts.intensiveintervention.org/ascreening on August 2, 2024.

National Reading Panel. (2000). *Teaching children to read: An evidence-based assessment of the scientific research literature on reading and its implications for reading instruction: Reports of the subgroups.* Accessed at https://www.nichd.nih.gov/sites/default/files/publications/pubs/nrp/Documents/report.pdf on August 2, 2024.

Ohio Department of Education & Workforce. (2024). *Use of high-quality literacy instructional and intervention materials in Ohio's elementary schools: Results from a statewide survey.* Columbus, OH: Author. Accessed at https://education.ohio.gov/getattachment/Topics/Learning-in-Ohio/English-Language-Art/Resources-for-English-Language-Arts/High-Quality-Instructional-Materials-in-English-La/HQIM-Survey-Results-Report.pdf.aspx?lang=en-US on August 2, 2024.

Paschler, H., Bain, P. M., Bottge, B. A., Graesser, A., Koedinger, K., McDaniel, M., et al. (2007, September) *Organizing instruction and study to improve student learning: IES practice guide.* Washington, DC: National Center for Education Research, Institute of Education Sciences, U.S. Department of Education. Accessed at https://files.eric.ed.gov/fulltext/ED498555.pdf on August 2, 2024.

Rathmann, K., Loter, K., & Vockert, T. (2020). Critical events throughout the educational career: the effect of grade retention and repetition on school-aged children's well-being. *International Journal of Environmental Research and Public Health, 17*(11), 4012.

The Reading League. (2022). *Science of reading: Defining guide.* Syracuse, NY: Author. Accessed at www.thereadingleague.org/wp-content/uploads/2022/03/Science-of-Reading-eBook-2022.pdf on January 10, 2025.

The Reading League (2023). *Curriculum evaluation guidelines.* Syracuse, NY: Author. Accessed at https://www.thereadingleague.org/wp-content/uploads/2023/03/The-Reading-League-Curriculum-Evaluation-Guidelines-2023.pdf on August 2, 2024.

Ringeisen, H., Henderson, K., & Hoagwood, K. (2003). Context matters: Schools and the "research to practice gap" in children's mental health. *School Psychology Review, 32*(2), 153–168.

Robinson, V. M. J., Lloyd, C. A., & Rowe, K. J. (2008). The impact of leadership on student outcomes: An analysis of the differential effects of leadership types. *Educational Administration Quarterly, 44*(5), 635–674. https://doi.org/10.1177/0013161X08321509

Rose, J. (2006, March). *Independent review of the teaching of early reading: Final report.* London, UK: Department for Education and Skills. Accessed at http://dera.ioe.ac.uk/5551/2/report.pdf on August 2, 2024.

Rosenshine, B. (2012). Principles of instruction: Research-based strategies that all teachers should know. *American Educator, 36*(1), 12–39.

Rowe, K. (2005). *Teaching reading: Report and recommendations.* Canberra, Australia: Department of Education, Science and Training. Accessed at https://research.acer.edu.au/cgi/viewcontent.cgi?article=1004&context=tll_misc on August 2, 2024.

Ruby, S. F., Crosby-Cooper, T., & Vanderwood, M. L. (2011). Fidelity of problem solving in everyday practice: Typical training may miss the mark. *Journal of Educational and Psychological Consultation, 21*(3), 233–258. https://doi.org/10.1080/10474412.2011.598017

Seidenberg, M. S. (2017). *Language at the speed of sight: how we read, why so many can't, and what can be done about it.* New York, Basic Books.

Simmons, D. C., & Kame'enui, E. J. (2003, March). A consumer's guide to evaluating a core reading program grades K–3: A critical elements analysis. Accessed at https://iris.peabody.vanderbilt.edu/wp-content/uploads/2013/06/cons_guide_instr.pdf on December 20, 2024.

Simmons, D. C., Kame'enui, E. J., Good, R. H., Harn, B., Cole, C. E., & Braun, D. (2000). Building, implementing, and sustaining a beginning reading model: School by school and lessons learned. *OSSC Bulletin, 43*(3). Accessed at https://eric.ed.gov/?id=ED443080 on January 10, 2025.

Simos, P. G., Fletcher, J. M., Sarkari, S., Billingsley, R. L., Denton, C., & Papanicolaou, A. C. (2007a). Altering the brain circuits for reading through intervention: A magnetic source imaging study. *Neuropsychology, 21*(4), 485–496. https://doi.org/10.1037/0894–4105.21.4.485

Simos, P. G., Fletcher, J. M., Sarkari, S., Billingsley-Marshall, R., Denton, C. A., & Papanicolaou, A. C. (2007b). Intensive instruction affects brain magnetic activity associated with reading fluency in children with dyslexia. *Journal of Learning Disabilities, 40*(1), 37–48. https://doi.org/10.1177/00222194070400010301

Simos, P. G., Fletcher, J. M., Sarkari, S., Billingsley, R. L., Francis, D. J., Castillo, E. M., et al. (2005). Early development of neurophysiological processes involved in normal reading and reading disability: A magnetic source imaging study. *Neuropsychology, 19*(6), 787–798. https://doi.org/10.1037/0894-4105.19.6.787

Smartt, S. M. (2020). Assessment basics. In M. C. Hougen & S. M. Smartt (Eds.), *Fundamentals of literacy instruction and assessment, pre-K–6* (2nd ed., pp. 34–41). Baltimore, MD: Brookes.

Snow, C. E., Burns, M. S., & Griffin, P. (1998). *Preventing reading difficulties in young children.* Washington, DC: National Research Council. Accessed at https://nap.nationalacademies.org/read/6023/chapter/1 on August 2, 2024.

Steffe, L. P., & Gale, J. (Eds.) (1995). *Constructivism in education.* New York: Routledge.

Stevens, E. A., Stewart, A., Vaughn, S., Lee, Y. R., Scammacca, N., & Swanson, E. (2024). The effects of a tier 2 reading comprehension intervention aligned to tier 1 instruction for fourth graders with inattention and reading difficulties. *Journal of School Psychology, 105*, 1–14. https://doi.org/10.1016/j.jsp.2024.101320

Strong-Wilson, T., & Ellis, J. (2007). Children and place: Reggio Emilia's environment as third teacher. *Theory Into Practice, 46*(1), 40–47. https://doi.org/10.1080/00405840709336547

Sugai, G., & Horner, R. H. (2006). A promising approach for expanding and sustaining school-wide positive behavior support. *School Psychology Review, 35*(2), 246–259. https://doi.org/10.1080/02796015.2006.12087989

Sweller, J. (2003). Evolution of human cognitive architecture. *The Psychology of Learning and Motivation, 43*, 215–266. https://doi.org/10.1016/S0079-7421(03)01015-6

Sweller, J. (2016). Cognitive load theory, evolutionary educational psychology, and instructional design. In D. C. Geary & D. B. Berch (Eds.), *Evolutionary perspectives on child development and education* (pp. 291–306). Springer International Publishing/Springer Nature.

Sweller, J., Mawer, R. F., & Howe, W. (1982). Consequences of history-cued and means–End strategies in problem solving. *The American Journal of Psychology, 95*(3), 455–483. https://doi.org/10.2307/1422136

Torgesen, J. K. (1998, February). *Individual differences in response to reading intervention* [Paper presentation]. Pacific Coast Research Conference, La Jolla, CA.

Torgesen, J. K. (2002). The prevention of reading difficulties. *Journal of School Psychology, 40*(1), 7–26. https://doi.org/10.1016/S0022-4405(01)00092-9

Torgesen, J. K. (2006). *A comprehensive K-3 reading assessment plan: Guidance for school leaders.* Portsmouth, NH: RMC Research Corporation, Center on Instruction. Accessed at https://www.azed.gov/sites/default/files/2016/11/K-3%20Comprehensive%20Assessment%20Plan.pdf?id=583c5306aadebe13d87d4201 on August 2, 2024.

Torgesen, J. K. (2009). The Response to Intervention instructional model: Some outcomes from a large-scale implementation in Reading First schools. *Child Development Perspectives, 3*(1), 38–40. https://doi.org/10.1111/j.1750-8606.2009.00073.x

Torgesen, J. K. & Burgess, S. R. (1998). Consistency of reading-related phonological processes throughout early childhood: Evidence from longitudinal-correlational and instructional studies. In J. L. Metsala & L. C. Ehri (Eds.), *Word recognition in beginning literacy* (pp. 161–188). Mahwah, NJ: Lawrence Erlbaum Associates.

Underwood, S. (2018). *What is the evidence for an uninterrupted, 90-minute literacy instruction block?* [Literacy brief]. Education Northwest. Accessed at https://educationnorthwest.org/sites/default/files/resources/uninterrupted-literacy-block-brief.pdf on August 2, 2024.

van Bergen, E., Hart, S. A., Latvala, A., Vuoksimaa, E., Tolvanen, A., & Torppa, M. (2022). Literacy skills seem to fuel literacy enjoyment, rather than vice versa. *Developmental Science, 26*(3), 1–11. https://doi.org/10.1111/desc.13325

Van Camp, A. M., Wehby, J. H., Martin, B. L. N., Wright, J. R., & Sutherland, K. S. (2020). Increasing opportunities to respond to intensify academic and behavioral interventions: A meta-analysis. *School Psychology Review, 49*(1), 31–46. https://doi.org/10.1080/2372966x.2020.1717369

Van Canegem, T., Van Houtte, M., & Demanet, J. (2022). Grade retention: A pathway to solitude? A cross-national multilevel analysis of the effects of being retained on students' sense of belonging. *Comparative Education Review, 66*(4), 664–687.

VanDerHeyden, A. M., & Burns, M. K. (2023). The instructional hierarchy: Connecting student learning and instruction. *Perspectives on Language and Literacy, 49*(1), 10–13.

van Dijk, W., Lane, H. B., & Gage, N. A. (2023). How do intervention studies measure the relation between implementation fidelity and students' reading outcomes? A systematic review. *The Elementary School Journal, 124*(1), 56–84. https://doi.org/10.1086/725672

Vaughn, S., Gersten, R., Dimino, J., Taylor, M. J., Newman-Gonchar, R., Krowka, S., et al. (2022). *Providing reading interventions for students in grades 4–9 (WWC 2022007)*. Washington, DC: National Center for Education Evaluation and Regional Assistance (NCEE), Institute of Education Sciences, U.S. Department of Education. Accessed at https://whatworks.ed.gov on December 20, 2024.

Vellutino, F. R., Scanlon, D. M., Zhang, H., & Schatschneider, C. (2008). Using response to kindergarten and first grade intervention to identify children at-risk for long-term reading difficulties. *Reading and Writing: An Interdisciplinary Journal, 21*(4), 437–480. https://doi.org/10.1007/s11145-007-9098-2

Walker, H. M., Horner, R. H., Sugai, G., Bullis, M., Sprague, J. R., Bricker, D., et al. (1996). Integrated approaches to preventing antisocial behavior patterns among school-age children and youth. *Journal of Emotional and Behavioral Disorders, 4*, 193–256.

Wannarka, R., & Ruhl, K. (2008). Seating arrangements that promote positive academic and behavioural outcomes: A review of empirical research. *Support for Learning, 23*(2), 90–93.

Wanzek, J., Stevens, E. A., Williams, K. J., Scammacca, N., Vaughn, S., & Sargent, K. (2018). Current evidence on the effects of intensive early reading interventions. *Journal of Learning Disabilities, 57*(4), 612–624. https://doi.org/10.1177/0022219418775110

Will, M. C. (1986). Educating children with learning problems: A shared responsibility. *Exceptional Children, 52*(5), 411–415. https://doi.org/10.1177/001440298605200502

Willingham, D. T. (2009). *Why don't students like school? A cognitive scientist answers questions about how the mind works and what it means for the classroom.* San Francisco: Jossey-Bass.

Willingham, D. T. (2023). *Outsmart your brain: Why learning is hard and how you can make it easy.* New York: Gallery Books.

Wolf, M., & Stoodley, C. J. (2007). *Proust and the squid: The story and science of the reading brain.* New York: HarperCollins.

Index

A

accuracy phase, 22–23
action plans, 59, 111
  "Building Leadership Team Action Plan," 107, 168
  data and, 89, 90–91
  "Grade-Level Team Action Plan," 89, 90, 162
  for Tier 1, 85, 89–91, 92–93
  Tier 2 and 3, 106–107
administrators, 2
agendas, meeting, 72–73
  "Building Leadership Team," 92, 106, 163–164
  "Building Leadership Team Agenda Outcome Analysis," 177–178
  data and, 75
  "Grade-Level Team Agenda Tier 1," 82, 84, 156–157
  "Grade-Level Team Agenda Tiers 2 and 3," 98, 99, 169–170
alignment, 30, 55, 57, 114
  of instruction with needs, 116
  intensification and, 113, 114
  intervention selection and, 103, 105
  of skills and sequencing of instruction, 16–17
"Allocating Adult Resources," 102, 150
Alternative Educational Delivery Systems: Enhancing Instructional Options for All Students (Graden, Zins, & Curtis), 48
Archer, A., 27, 28
assessment, 32–43
  "Building Reading Test Review" reproducible, 135–136
  choosing tests, 36–43
  "District Reading Test Plan" reproducible, 137–138
  impactful systems of, 50, 51, 85, 88
  importance of, 33–35
  instructionally relevant, 33, 35
  leveraging indicators of proficiency and, 33, 34–35
  "Our Programs" reproducible, 140–141
  outcome, 37, 42–43
  progress monitoring and, 37, 42
  purposes of, 35–36
  questions guiding, 33, 34
  "Reading Tests Used" reproducible, 133–134
  "Reasons We Assess" reproducible, 139
  streamlining, 75
  targeting student needs using, 99–101
  Tier 1 and, 85, 88
  Tier 2 and 3, 99–101
  types of and gap analysis, 40–41
  validity of, 37, 38, 39, 42
  wrong kinds of, 48, 49

B

balanced literacy approaches, 1
barriers to success, 2, 60–61
behaviorist approaches, 20
beliefs, core, 47
brain
  memory and, 21
  reading and, 11, 12
Brown, B., 89
"Building Leadership Team Action Plan," 107, 168

"Building Leadership Team Agenda," 92, 106, 163–164
"Building Leadership Team Agenda Outcome Analysis," 177–178
"Building Leadership Team Protocol Gap Analysis," 106–107, 167
"Building Leadership Team Protocol Gap Identification," 92, 106, 165–166
"Building Leadership Team Protocol Outcome Analysis," 181
building leadership teams, 67, 68, 69
   action planning, 92–93
   gap analysis, 92
   outcome review, 92
   Tier 1 conversations for, 92–93
   Tier 2 and 3, 106–107
"Building Reading Test Review," 36, 135–136

C

CATs. *See* computer adaptive tests (CATs)
CBM. *See* curriculum-based measures (CBM)
celebrations, 109, 111–112, 114, 121, 154
change
   levers for, 2, 49–59
   making it stick, 1–7
   supporting lasting, 119
choral reading, 28
choral responding, 27, 28
clarity, 54
   in lesson opening, 24, 25
   Tier 1, 89
classroom management, 85, 88
classroom organization, 24
Cloze reading, 28
collaboration, 65–66. *See also* teams
   culture of, 65
   definition of, 58
Collaborative Improvement Cycle, 5, 50, 58–62
   assessment and, 34
   implementation plans and, 66–67
   outcome analysis and, 109–113
   steps in, 59
   teams and, 65, 66, 73
   "Teams and the," 148
   Tier 1 gap analysis and, 84–85
   Tier 2 and 3 gap analysis, 99, 101
   Tiers 2 and 3, 98
collective efficacy, 65, 66
communication
   of student outcomes, 75, 76
   "Team Communication Plan," 147
   teams and, 69–71
"Comparing Intensity," 115–116, 153
complexity, breaking down in instruction, 24, 26
comprehension, 11, 13–17
computer adaptive tests (CATs), 37–38
consensus, 75–76
consistency. *See* fidelity
consonant-vowel-consonant (CVC) words, 26, 53, 102
construct validity, 39
constructivist approaches, 19–20
Consumer's Guide to Evaluating a Core Reading Program (Simmons & Kame'enui), 55–56
content
   presenting new, 24–25
   sequencing purposefully, 24, 26
context
   aligning local, 6
   new initiatives and, 2
core reading programs, 51
cumulative and distributed practice, 27
curriculum, 15–16
   materials for Tier 1, 85, 86–88
curriculum-based measures (CBM), 35, 37–38, 42

D

Dare to Lead (Brown), 89
data
   action planning and, 89, 90–91
   additional sources for Tier 3, 104–105
   aggregate, 60–61
   building leadership teams and, 92–93
   choosing tests and, 35–43
   considering types of, 41–42
   decision making based on, 58
   driving Tier 1 instruction with, 81–94
   driving Tier 2 and 3 instruction with, 96–107
   for gap analysis, 40–41
   gap analysis with, 99–101
   protocols, 110
   resistance to using as instruction driver, 75–76

sample protocols, 100
system-level uses of, 4–5
using student and educator, 110–111
decision making
data-based, 58, 61–62
data-based, modeling, 75
decisions
about materials, 16–18
de-implementation of old practices, 2, 54, 55, 75, 142
diagnostic assessments, 35–36, 37, 38–41
student-level, 39
system-level, 39–40
discovery learning. *See* minimally guided approaches
"District Reading Test Plan," 36, 137–138
dosage, 115–116
Dunn, S., 5

E

echo reading, 28
Educating Students With Learning Problems: A Shared Responsibility (Will), 48
The Education of All Handicapped Children Act, 47–48
"Elements of Explicit Instruction," 29, 131–132
engagement, 88
promoting active, 24, 26–27
explicit instruction, 11
"Elements of," 29, 131–132
fully guided approaches and, 20–21
Explicit Instruction: Effective and Efficient Teaching (Archer & Hughes), 27, 28

F

families, 2
data discussions with, 76
feedback, in effective instruction, 24, 27, 28
Feldman, K., 88
fidelity, 2
instructional environment and, 24
in Tier 1, 87–88
Tier 2 and 3, 104
fluency, 14–15
letter naming, 35
letter sound, 35
nonsense word, 35
oral reading, 34, 35

fluency phase, 22–23
Foster-Fishman, P. G., 5
fully guided approaches, 20–22

G

gap analysis, 40, 59
"Building Leadership Team Protocol Gap Analysis," 167
"Building Leadership Team Protocol Gap Identification," 165–166
building leadership teams and, 92
on Collaborative Improvement Cycle, 84–85
data types for, 40–41
on effective and equitable supports, 85–88
"Grade-Level Team Protocol Tiers 2 and 3 Gap Identification," 171–172
"Grade-Level Team Tiers 2 and 3 Gap Analysis," 173–174
on strategic leadership and teaming, 84, 85
for Tier 1, 84–89, 92
Tier 2 and 3, 99–101, 105–107
gap identification, 59
leadership team protocol for, 165–166
team protocol for, 92, 106, 165–166
Tier 1, 158–159
Tier 2 and 3, 97–98, 99, 106–107, 171–172
general outcome measures (GOMs), 37–38
generalization and transfer phase, 22–23
GOMs. *See* general outcome measures (GOMs)
Good Behavior Game, 88
Gough, P. B., 13
"Grade-Level Team Action Plan," 89, 90, 162
"Grade-Level Team Agenda Tier 1," 82, 84, 156–157
"Grade-Level Team Agenda Tiers 2 and 3," 98, 99, 169–170
"Grade-Level Team Protocol Tier 1 Gap Analysis," 82–83, 84, 160–161
"Grade-Level Team Protocol Tier 1 Gap Identification," 158–159
"Grade-Level Team Protocol Tiers 2 and 3 Gap Identification," 99, 171–172
"Grade-Level Team Tiers 2 and 3 Gap Analysis," 173–174
grade-level teams, 67, 68, 81–91
action planning by, 89–91
conversations for, 81–91

current reading outcomes reviews by, 82–83
gap analysis by, 84–89, 99
Graden, J. L., 48
group size, 114
grouping, 102–106
growth levels, student, 111–113
guided practice, 27
Guided Reading, 22

H

Hosp, J. L., 40
Hosp, M. K., 40
Howell, K. W., 40
Hughes, C., 27, 28

I

IATs. *See* intervention assistance teams (IATs)
implementation science, 2
implementation support, 6
implicit instruction, 11
improvement efforts, 108–117
  analyzing results of, 109–110
  intensifying system supports and, 113–115
  lessons learned in, 115–117
  student and educator data in, 110–111
  summarizing system-level outcomes and, 111–113
inquiry learning. *See* minimally guided approaches
instruction. *See also* reading instruction
  data as driver for, 75–76
  elements of effective, 23–29
  fully guided approaches, 20–22
  hierarchy in, 22–23
  minimally guided approaches, 20, 21–22
  scheduling, 56
  strategies for Tier 1, 85, 86–88
instructional hierarchy, 22–23, 27–28
  Tier 1 and, 87
instructional matches, 114
instructional strategies, 113
intelligence tests, 35
intensification, 108–117
  alignment and, 113, 114
  lessons learned in, 115–117
intervention assistance teams (IATs), 48–49
intervention programs, 51, 53
"Intervention Scheduling," 104, 152
intervention selection, 102–103
"Intervention Selection Considerations," 103, 151
interventions
  "Comparing Intensity" reproducible, 153
  early, 17, 20
  prevention *vs.*, 11, 13
  system-level implementation of, 4–5
  team-based planning for, 60–61
interview assessments, 40

L

language comprehension, 11, 13
Lead to Succeed
  on aligning across tiers, 53–54
  on aligning professional learning, 29–30
  on considering types of data, 41–42
  on effective communication, 70–71
  on intensification, 114–115
  on skill instruction, 16–17
  on Tier 1 gap analysis, 90–91
  on Tier 2 and 3 gap analysis, 105–106
leaders
  building teams and, 67, 68
  district teams and, 67, 68
  gap analysis and, 84, 85
  as lever for change, 50, 58
  role of in instruction, 29–30
  Tier 2 and 3 gap analysis, 99, 101
leadership teams
  building, 6–7
  "Building Leadership Team Action Plan," 107, 168
  "Building Leadership Team Agenda," 92, 106, 163–164
  "Building Leadership Team Agenda Outcome Analysis," 177–178
  "Building Leadership Team Protocol Gap Analysis," 167
  "Building Leadership Team Protocol Gap Identification," 165–166
  "Building Leadership Team Protocol Outcome Analysis," 181
learning
  all children's ability for, 47
  instructional hierarchy and, 22–23
  in minimally *vs.* fully guided approaches, 21–22
lesson openers, 24, 25

letter naming fluency, 35
letter sound fluency, 35
levers for change, 2, 49–59
   Collaborative Improvement Cycle, 50, 58–62
   effective and equitable tiered supports, 50, 51–56
   impactful assessment system, 50, 51
   strategic leadership and teaming, 50, 58
   targeted professional learning, 50, 56–57
   Tier 1 gap analysis and, 85

M

mastery, practicing to, 24, 27–28
materials, 1–2, 113
   assessment and, 40, 41
   choosing, 23
   intensification and, 113–116
   making decisions about, 16–18
   support tiers and, 51, 52, 54, 55
   teams and, 67, 68, 70–71
   Tier 1, 85, 86–88, 89, 90
meetings
   "Building Leadership Team Action Plan," 107, 168
   "Building Leadership Team Agenda," 92, 106, 163–164
   "Building Leadership Team Agenda Outcome Analysis," 177–178
   "Building Leadership Team Protocol Gap Analysis," 167
   "Building Leadership Team Protocol Gap Identification," 165–166
   facilitation of team, 71–73
   "Grade-Level Team Action Plan," 89, 90, 162
   "Grade-Level Team Agenda Outcome Analysis," 175–176
   "Grade-Level Team Agenda Tier 1," 82, 84, 156–157
   "Grade-Level Team Agenda Tiers 2 and 3," 98, 99, 169–170
   "Grade-Level Team Protocol Outcome Analysis," 179–180
   "Grade-Level Team Protocol Tier 1 Gap Analysis," 160–161
   "Grade-Level Team Tiers 2 and 3 Gap Analysis," 173–174
   guide for, 6, 123, 155–182
   "Team Growth Reflection," 182
memory, 21

minimally guided approaches, 20, 21–22
minority students, 48
MLLs. *See* multilingual learners (MLLs)
MTSS. *See* multitiered system of support (MTSS)
MTSS in the Science of Reading: Defining Guide (The Reading League), 3
"MTSS World Café," 121, 154
multilingual learners (MLLs), 5, 17
   gap identification and, 97–98, 114–115
   instructional routines and, 87
   team representation for, 69
   Tier 3 interventions and, 117
multitiered system of support (MTSS), 2–4
   assessment and, 32–43
   core beliefs underlying, 47
   definition of, 3
   effective instruction and, 18–30
   engineering a robust, 45–76
   foundations of, 47–62
   improving and intensifying, 108–117
   leader toolkit for, 123, 125–154
   levers for change in, 49–59
   meeting guide for, 123, 155–182
   model of, 50
   origins of, 47–49
   research on, 11
   system-level implementation of, 4–5
   teams in, 64–76

N

National Academy of Sciences, 48
National Association of School Psychologists, 48
National Reading Panel, 49
National Research Council, 49
95 Percent Group, 89
nonsense word fluency, 35
Nowell, B., 5

O

observation assessments, 40
Office of Special Education and Rehabilitative Services, 48
oral language, 17
"Our Programs," 53, 140–141
"Our Teams," 66, 68, 143
outcome analysis, 59, 109–113

outcomes
    assessments for, 35–36, 37, 42–43
    "Building Leadership Team Agenda Outcome Analysis," 92, 106, 177–178
    "Building Leadership Team Protocol Outcome Analysis," 181
    building leadership teams and, 92
    data driving Tier 1 instruction and, 85, 86–88
    "Grade-Level Team Agenda Outcome Analysis," 175–176
    "Grade-Level Team Protocol Outcome Analysis," 179–180
    improving, 79–117
    summarizing system-level, 111–113
    Tier 1 and, 85, 86–88, 92
overidentification, 83

P

parents. *See* families
partner practice, 112
partner responding, 27, 28
phonemic awareness, 14–15
phonics, 14–15
practice to mastery, 24, 27–28
prevention
    fully guided approaches and, 20
    MTSS effectiveness in, 61
    possibility and effectiveness of, 11, 13
problem solving, 21
    collaborative, 58
    moving beyond student-level, 49
problem-based learning. *See* minimally guided approaches
processing speed, 35
professional learning and development, 29–30, 75, 104
    targeting, 50, 56–57
    Tier 1 and, 85, 88–89
    Tier 2 and 3 gap analysis, 99, 101
proficiency, leveraging indicators of, 33, 34–35
programs
    audits for, 55, 142
    choosing, 55
    core reading, 51, 55
    intervention, 51, 53
    "Our Programs" reproducible, 53, 140–141
    supplemental, 51
progress monitoring, 34–35, 76
    assessments for, 35–36, 37, 42
    Tier 2 and 3, 98
prompted practice, 27

R

reading
    essential skills for, 14–15
    skill in and enjoyment of, 12
Reading and Writing Workshop, 22
reading comprehension, 13–17
    definition of, 13
Reading First, 49
reading improvement
    making it stick, 1–7
    scenarios on, 119–121
    science of reading and, 1–4
    systems-level, 4–5
    teams in supporting, 64–76
reading instruction, 18–30
    design and delivery of, 23–29
    effectiveness assessment of, 60–61
    fully guided approaches, 20–22
    leader's role in, 29–30
    minimally guided approaches, 20, 21–22
    new information presentation in, 24–25
    research on, 19–20
    Tier 1, 80–94
    Tier 2 and 3, 96–107
"Reading Instruction and Intervention Program Audit," 55, 142
The Reading League, 3, 55
"Reading MTSS Reflection Guide," 50, 126–130
reading science, 1–4, 5–6
    assessment and, 32–43
    Collaborative Improvement Cycle and, 59–62
    on comprehension, 11, 13
    definition of, 3
    effective instruction and, 18–30
    instructional hierarchy and, 22–23
    on prevention, 11, 13
    reading as natural *vs.* not natural, 11, 12
    research on, 11–17
    understanding, 10, 18, 32
"Reading Tests Used," 36, 133–134

"Reasons We Assess," 38, 39, 139
reflection, xii
  on assessment, 32
  on effective instruction, 18
  on foundational skills, 10
  on improvement and intensification, 108
  on MTSS, 46
  "MTSS World Café" for, 121
  "Reading MTSS Reflection Guide," 6–7, 126–130
  "Team Growth Reflection," 182
  on teams, 64
  on Tier I instruction, 80
  on Tiers 2 and 3 instruction, 96
  on training/coaching needs, 17
reproducibles
  "Allocating Adult Resources," 150
  "Building Leadership Team Action Plan," 168
  "Building Leadership Team Agenda," 163–164
  "Building Leadership Team Agenda Outcome Analysis," 177–178
  "Building Leadership Team Protocol Gap Analysis," 167
  "Building Leadership Team Protocol Gap Identification," 165–166
  "Building Leadership Team Protocol Outcome Analysis," 181
  "Building Reading Test Review," 135–136
  "Comparing Intensity," 153
  "District Reading Test Plan," 137–138
  "Grade-Level Team Action Plan," 162
  "Grade-Level Team Agenda Outcome Analysis," 175–176
  "Grade-Level Team Agenda Tier 1," 156–157
  "Grade-Level Team Agenda Tiers 2 and 3," 169–170
  "Grade-Level Team Protocol Outcome Analysis," 179–180
  "Grade-Level Team Protocol Tier 1 Gap Analysis," 160–161
  "Grade-Level Team Protocol Tier 1 Gap Identification," 158–159
  "Grade-Level Team Protocol Tiers 2 and 3 Gap Identification," 171–172
  "Grade-Level Team Tiers 2 and 3 Gap Analysis," 173–174
  "Intervention Scheduling," 152
  "Intervention Selection Considerations," 151
  MTSS meeting guide, 123, 155–182
  "MTSS World Café," 154
  "Our Programs," 140–141
  "Our Teams," 143
  "Reading Instruction and Intervention Program Audit," 142
  "Reading MTSS Reflection Guide," 126–130
  "Reading Tests Used," 133–134
  "Reasons We Assess," 139
  "Team Communication Plan," 147
  "Team Growth Reflection," 182
  "Teams and the Collaborative Improvement Cycle," 148
  "Tier 1 Discussion," 149
research
  applying, 17
  intervention selection and, 103
  on learning, 21
  on minimally and fully guided approaches, 21–22
  on oral reading fluency, 34
  on reading instruction, 19–20
  reading science, 11–17
resources
  allocating, 102
  "Allocating Adult Resources," 150
response boards, 28
response to intervention (RTI), 4, 49, 50
retention, 12
review assessments, 40
Rights Without Labels, 48
room arrangement, 24
routines, 89
RTI. *See* response to intervention (RTI)

S

scenarios, 119–121
scheduling, 55–56
  "Intervention Scheduling" reproducible for, 152
  sample schedules for, 56, 57
  team meetings, 82–83
  for Tier 1, 85, 86
  Tier 2 and 3, 103–104
  time to team, 73–75
science of reading. *See* reading science
scope, 24, 26

screening, 34–35
  assessments for, 35–36, 37–38
  reviewing for Tier 1, 82
  Tier 2 and 3, 98
sequence, 24, 26
silent signals, 27, 28
"Simple View of Reading" (Gough & Tunmer), 13
skills
  alignment and sequencing of instruction, 16–17
  essential reading, 14–15
  focus on, 17
  grouping based on, 102–106
  integration across, 17
  prioritizing, 11, 13
  reading enjoyment and, 12
  reciprocity among, 14, 15
  sequence of essential, 15–17
special education, 48
staggered interventions, 56
standardization, of assessment administration, 37, 42–43. *See also* fidelity
standards, 15–16
strategic planning, collaborative, 58
student-centered approaches, 19–20
student-directed instruction. *See* minimally guided approaches
student-level teams, 68
supplemental reading programs, 51
system supports, intensifying, 113–115

T

"Team Communication Plan," 71, 72, 147
"Team Growth Reflection," 112, 182
"Team Review," 69, 144–146
teams, 64–76
  "Allocating Adult Resources," 150
  "and the Collaborative Improvement Cycle," 148
  assessments and, 36
  "Building Leadership Team Agenda," 92, 106, 163–164
  "Building Leadership Team Protocol Gap Analysis," 167
  "Building Leadership Team Protocol Outcome Analysis," 181
  building-leadership, 68
  Collaborative Improvement Cycle and, 73
  common challenges and solutions for, 73–76
  communication and, 69–71
  district-leadership, 68
  functions of, 66–73
  grade-level, 67, 68, 81–91
  "Grade-Level Team Agenda Outcome Analysis," 175–176
  "Grade-Level Team Agenda Tiers 2 and 3," 98, 99, 169–170
  "Grade-Level Team Protocol Outcome Analysis," 179–180
  "Grade-Level Team Protocol Tiers 2 and 3 Gap Identification," 171–172
  importance on in reading change, 65–66
  intervention assistance, 48–49
  as lever for change, 50, 58
  meeting facilitation for, 71–73
  membership in, 69
  "Our Teams" reproducible, 66, 143
  stakeholders in, 54–55
  student-level, 68
  "Team Review" reproducible, 144–146
  Tier 2 and 3 gap analysis, 99, 101
  types of, 67–68
"Teams and the Collaborative Improvement Cycle," 73, 148
terminology, 53
tests, 40. *See also* assessment
Tier 1, 81–94
  action planning for, 85, 89–91
  action plans for, 85, 88, 89–91
  building leadership teams and, 92–93
  current reading outcomes review and, 82–83
  "Discussion" reproducible, 149
  effective and equitable supports in, 85–88
  fidelity in, 87–88
  gap analysis, 84–89
  gap analysis for, 84–89
  grade-level team conversations for, 81–91
  "Grade-Level Team Protocol Tier 1 Gap Analysis," 160–161
  "Grade-Level Team Protocol Tier 1 Gap Identification," 158–159
  instruction strategies for, 85, 86–88
  intensification of, 114–115

key features of, 52
"Tier 1 Discussion" reproducible, 82, 149
Tier 2, 96–107
  action planning, 106
  gap analysis, 99–101
  gap identification, 97–98
  "Grade-Level Team Agenda Tiers 2 and 3," 98, 99, 169–170
  "Grade-Level Team Protocol Tiers 2 and 3 Gap Identification," 171–172
  grouping, 102–106
  instructional sequence, 101
  scheduling, 103–104
Tier 3, 96–107
  action planning, 106
  gap analysis, 99–101
  gap identification, 97–98
  "Grade-Level Team Protocol Tiers 2 and 3 Gap Identification," 171–172
  grouping, 102–106
  instructional sequence, 101
  intensification in, 116–117
  intentionality in, 116–117
  key features of, 52
  scheduling, 103–104
  special design considerations for, 104–106
tiered supports, 50, 51–56
time, 113
toolkit, MTSS, 6, 123, 125–154
  "Allocating Adult Resources," 150
  "Building Reading Test Review," 135–136
  "Comparing Intensity," 153
  "District Reading Test Plan," 137–138
  "Elements of Explicit Instruction," 131–132
  "Intervention Scheduling," 152
  "Intervention Selection Considerations," 151
  "MTSS World Café," 154
  "Our Programs," 140–141
  "Our Teams," 143
  "Reading Instruction and Intervention Program Audit," 142
  "Reading MTSS Reflection Guide," 126–130
  "Reading Tests Used," 133–134
  "Reasons We Assess," 139
  "Team Communication Plan," 147
  "Team Review," 144–146
  "Teams and the Collaborative Improvement Cycle," 148
training, 17
  on assessment data, 75
  meeting facilitator, 72
Tunmer, W. E., 13

U

universal screening, 1
U.S. Department of Education, 48

V

validity, 37, 38, 39, 42
visual-spatial reasoning, 35
vocabulary, 14–15

W

Will, M. C., 48
word recognition, 11, 13
  definition of, 13
  instructional hierarchy and, 22–23
  sample lesson framework on, 25
written responses, 28

Y

Yang, H., 5

Implement With IMPACT
Jenice Pizzuto and Steven Carney
Learn how to build an implementation team that will bridge the implementation gap and prevent the adopt-and-abandon cycle that often comes with change. The IMPACT framework provides distinct stages and human- and learning-centered design elements to help you achieve quick, tangible wins and sustainable, scalable results.
BKG093

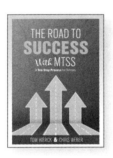

The Road to Success With MTSS
Tom Hierck and Chris Weber
Packed with research-based strategies, *The Road to Success With MTSS* is an essential road map for educators beginning their school's multitiered system of supports (MTSS) journey and those who have already come so far and are looking to reflect and reset for success.
BKG084

It's Possible!
Pati Montgomery and Angela Hanlin
Based on research regarding how to improve outcomes for students and highly effective schools, leaders, including principals, now have a reliable guide to ensure universal literacy instruction while supporting their teachers and increasing reading proficiency for all students.
BKG161

Read Alouds for All Learners
Molly Ness
In *Read Alouds for All Learners: A Comprehensive Plan for Every Subject, Every Day, Grades PreK–8*, Molly Ness provides a compelling case for the integration, or reintegration, of the read aloud in schools and a step-by-step resource for preK–8 educators in classrooms.
BKG116

Solving the Literacy Puzzle
Norene A. Bunt
Using graphic organizers, assessments, and reflection questions, educators can unpack five core components of literacy instruction within the science of reading framework. This comprehensive guide prepares teachers to confidently implement effective literacy instruction in their classrooms.
BKG158

Solution Tree | Press

Visit SolutionTree.com or call 800.733.6786 to order.

We don't just help schools make a change, we help them *be* the change

REAL IMPACT. RELEVANT SOLUTIONS. RESULTS-DRIVEN APPROACH.

From funding to faculty retention, the evolving demands schools face can be overwhelming. That's where we come in. With professional development rooted in decades of research and delivered by many of the educators who literally wrote the book on it, we empower schools to achieve meaningful change with real, sustainable results.

The change starts here. We can make it happen together.

See how we can get real results for your school or district.

Scan the code or visit:

SolutionTree.com/Results-Driven

 Solution Tree

LET'S SEE WHAT WE CAN DO TOGETHER